PROJECTS FOR
YOUNG SCIENTISTS

ECOLOGY

BY MARTIN J.
GUTNIK

A GROLIER COMPANY

FRANKLIN WATTS, INC.
NEW YORK I LONDON I TORONTO I SYDNEY

DEDICATED TO
SALLY GUTNIK
MY MOM

Diagrams courtesy of Vantage Art.
Photographs courtesy of: NASA: opposite p. 1;
Clayborn Benson: p. 12; U.S. Geological Survey:
p. 30; United Nations: p. 54; U.S. Forest Service:
p. 82; Enrico Ferorelli/Wheeler Pictures: p. 108.

Library of Congress Cataloging in Publication Data

Gutnik, Martin J.
Ecology.

(Projects for young scientists)
Includes index.
Summary: A collection of environmental science
projects which demonstrate the delicate balance
of ecological systems and how both people and
nature can destroy this balance.
1. Ecology—Experiments—Juvenile literature.
(1. Ecology—Experiments. 2. Science—Experiments.
3. Experiments.) I. Title. II. Series.
QH541.24.G87   1984   551.5′072   83-27381
ISBN 0-531-15128-X (paper ed.)
ISBN 0-531-04765-2 (lib. bdg.)

PART I.
INTRODUCTION 1

What Is Ecology? 1
The Biosphere 2
Biomes of the Earth 4
Ecosystems 8
Food Webs 9

PART II.
WHAT IS A SCIENCE PROJECT? 13

The Scientific Method 13
How to Apply to Science Fairs 17
Identifying an Environmental Project 18
How to Set Up and
Present Your Science Project 19
Demonstration of the Science Project
at a Science Fair 27
The Formal Report 27

PART III.
PROJECTS ON AIR 29

The Makeup of Air 29

Pollutants in the Air 31
Volcanic Pollution of the Air 32
Forest Fires and Their Role in
Naturally Polluting the Air 36
Automobile Emissions and
Particulates in the Air 38
Auto Emissions, Convection, Temperature
Inversions, and Photochemical Smog 45
Other Projects on Air 50

PART IV.
PROJECTS ON WATER 53

A Moisture-Gradient Box 53
Succession 58
River Ecosystems 65
The Effects of Municipalities and
Industry on Water 72
Pesticides and Water Pollution 77
Other Projects on Water 80

PART V.
PROJECTS ON SOIL AND
TERRESTRIAL ECOSYSTEMS 83

The Makeup of Soil 83
Project on Resource Use—Recycling Paper 88
An Environmental System 92
Observations and Experiments
for the Environmental System 99
Other Projects on Ecosystems 103
Biological Clocks in Plants and Animals 104
Photoperiodic Projects at Fairs 106

PART VI.
HUMAN POPULATION AND THE ENVIRONMENT 107

GLOSSARY 112
INDEX 119

ECOLOGY

PROJECTS FOR
YOUNG SCIENTISTS

1

INTRODUCTION

The study of ecology is a lengthy process. It has taken people many years to comprehend what has been happening to the environment, and it will probably take many years more to correct these problems. But the first step is understanding.

The projects in this book demonstrate various aspects of the natural order and the profound effect that people have had on nature. These projects weave through ecological concepts and, in the end, should leave the reader with a clear understanding of natural cycles.

All the experiments herein are designed to demonstrate how ecological systems and spheres operate and how both nature and people can destroy the delicate balances of them. Many of these experiments are quite sophisticated and potentially dangerous if special care is not taken by the experimenter. All the experiments will be accompanied by the proper procedures for safe performance.

WHAT IS ECOLOGY?

Ecology is the study of how all living things interrelate with one another and their nonliving environment. The planet Earth is an assemblage of plant and animal species inhabiting a common area, the *biosphere*, and, therefore, having a profound effect on one another and on their nonliving surroundings.

THE BIOSPHERE

All life on Earth exists within the biosphere. There are two major parts to the biosphere, the physical and the biological. Both are necessary for life support.

The physical (inorganic, or nonliving) part consists of soil, water, air, and light energy. Soil consists of rocks, gravel, sand, clay, mud, muck, and decaying organic materials. It has the ability to contain and support life. A major percentage of insects spend part of their life cycle in the soil. Vegetation depends on the soil for its nutrients. The soil is the Earth's medium for growth.

Water is the liquid portion of the biosphere, and it is everywhere. The amount of water present determines which type of biotic (living) community will form. Where water is abundant, we have forests. If water is scarce, we have deserts.

Water travels throughout the biosphere via the hydrologic cycle. The life-giving liquid bubbles up from underground springs and forms lakes, which in turn give birth to creeks, streams, and rivers. These serpentine ribbons of liquid cascade and meander to the oceans, where they meet the tides. Ocean currents, in turn, carry water from the Gulf of Mexico to England, from South America to Alaska.

As the sun radiates energy to the Earth, it causes surface water and vapor (given off by plants in a process called *transpiration*) to rise into the air as a gas. This is *evaporation*. As this water rises, it cools and condenses into clouds. These clouds are transported by wind to all parts of the biosphere. Laden with moisture, they drop their loads in the form of rain, snow, sleet, or hail. This is *precipitation*.

The atmosphere, which contains the gases necessary

for the metabolism of life, fills every space available. This shroud of gases that rises 600 miles (960 km) above the planet's surface also protects organisms from the harmful rays of the sun.

Air travels the globe on jet streams powered by the sun. It swirls about high- and low-pressure weather systems and rises and falls in convection currents determined by temperature.

The principal source of energy for the biosphere is sunlight. Green plants, in a process called *photosynthesis*, convert light energy into chemical energy and then into glucose, a simple sugar. This is done in accordance with the First Law of Thermodynamics, which states: Energy cannot be created or destroyed but can be transferred and transformed. Plants store the glucose, which is then transferred to other organisms within the biotic community through the food web.

Thus, all life on Earth depends upon solar energy for its existence. This leads us to the Second Law of Thermodynamics: In any transfer of energy from one form to another, some energy always escapes from the system. Energy is diluted with every transfer. Most forms of energy within the biosphere are transformed forms of solar energy.

The biological, or organic, part of the biosphere includes all life forms. All biotic communities consist of these basic components: the *autotrophic*, organisms that fix energy from the sun and manufacture glucose; and the *heterotrophic*, organisms that utilize the food stored by the autotrophs. Autotrophs are found in the areas of the community that are most exposed to light energy, while heterotrophic organisms are found closer to the ground, in the lower strata.

The place where any organism lives, that is, the space it occupies, is referred to as its *habitat*. All organisms have specific habitats where they can fulfill their biological function. What the organism does—its job, so to speak—is referred to as its *niche*. Some species occupy a broad biological niche, while others are more specialized. In the community, the total mass of living organisms is referred to as the *biomass*.

BIOMES OF THE EARTH

The biosphere is divided into major biotic communities, composed of all the plants, animals, and ecosystems of a large geographical region. The *biome* is a system of climax (mature) communities of plants and animals. All biomes possess similarities: climate, geography, and plant and animal life forms.

The *desert biome*, represented on every major continent, is usually located between mountains and grasslands. Deserts are characterized by low or scattered precipitation throughout the year. All deserts have sandy, loose soil.

Desert plants are called *xerophytes*, which means they require very little water. There are three types of desert plants: those that store water in their tissues, encysting the liquid beneath thick, waxy skins; shrubs with roots that penetrate deep into the soil to obtain water (these plants have the unique ability to lose their leaves during a dry spell and remain dormant until the next rain); and wildflowers and grasses, which appear only after a rain and go through their entire cycle within a few weeks.

Most animals of the desert are specially adapted to conserve water. The insects and reptiles each have a thick outer skin, which minimizes the loss of water through evaporation. Most of the mammals are nocturnal and do not usually drink water. They obtain liquid from the food they eat.

The *temperate deciduous forest biome* consists mainly of trees that shed their leaves each autumn. This biome, usually found between grasslands and the northern coniferous forests, is characterized by a rich organic soil result-

Biomes of North and South America

Grassland, Prairie, Plain

Desert

Coniferous Forest

Tundra

Deciduous Forest

Tropical Rain Forest

ing from the decomposition of the fallen leaves. The community experiences moderate temperatures during the growing season and harsh, cold winters with abundant snow. The precipitation is about the same throughout the year.

Due to the falling of the leaves, the forest is subject to variable light conditions, depending on the season. This variance in light allows for the development of several different layers of growth. Thus, the deciduous forest, with its abundance of niches and habitats, has a varied and productive animal community.

Belting the Earth at the equator, *tropical rain forests* form the most productive biome within the biosphere. Marked by 80 or more inches (200 cm) of rain and little variance in temperature, this biome displays more varieties of plant and animal species than any other.

Most life within the rain forest exists within the canopy, or cover, of trees. Due to the deluge of precipitation, the trees grow so large and thick that very little light can penetrate the canopy. If you were to walk the floor of a tropical rain forest, you would find the huge trunks of the gigantic trees; a moist, spongy soil; and very little air movement.

The *Arctic tundra* caps the Northern Hemisphere. The region has long, cold winters and short summers with moderate to cool temperatures. Precipitation comes mostly in the form of snow. There is very little precipitation in the summer. Yet during the summer the soil is constantly wet and soggy, due to a low evaporation rate and a permafrost layer (where the ground is permanently frozen) 6 inches (15.2 cm) beneath the surface.

The vegetation in this area is low-growing in order to protect itself from the cold and the mantle of snow. All trees and shrubs are dwarfed. Plant life consists mainly of grasses, sedges, and lichens. All the plants complete their growing cycles during the very short summer.

Most of the wildlife in the tundra is migratory, but there

are some permanent residents who remain active throughout the year. Some of these are the polar bear, musk ox, Arctic fox, and wolf. Tundra animals feed voraciously during the summer months, and, during the winter, they depend upon the layers of fat put on in the summer. Also during the summer months, the tundra has a high percentage of the Earth's waterfowl. The marshlike soil not only serves these water birds, it also hosts a myriad of insect life.

The *coniferous taiga,* or *boreal forest biome* forms the timberline that serves as the southern border of the tundra. This biome is characterized by evergreen trees, mostly spruce, pine, fir, and hemlock, and covers parts of North America, Europe, and Asia. The boreal forest is also a region of long, cold winters and short summers, but because there is no permafrost, trees can develop.

Due to the nature of the forest, the soil is of very poor quality. Needles and other debris from the trees fall and decay slowly on the forest floor. During the process of decomposition, they form a weak acid, which leaches nutritive minerals from the soil.

Squirrels, birds, and insects feed upon the bounties of this forest. Larger rodents, greatly dependent on a low-growing shrub layer, cannot live in it. Deer are plentiful, and elk and caribou can be found in the northern regions of this biome. Foxes, wolves, hawks, and many other predators are abundant, feeding upon the snowshoe hare and mice.

The *grassland* community can be found between forests and deserts on every continent. These vast expanses of flat lands experience 25 to 30 inches (63.5 to 76.2 cm) of rain annually but are subject to long periods of drought. The vegetation, such as buffalo grass, survives by developing specific adaptations to the climatic trends of the biome. Yet, even with these adaptations, after long periods of drought, the vegetational composition of these prairies changes.

Grassland biomes experience cold, harsh winters and long, hot summers. The animals of this community must be hardy and well adapted to long periods of little food.

Within the mulch (a thick layer of plants that remains at ground level) lives a thriving community of insects, including beetles, spiders, ants, grasshoppers, crickets, leafhoppers, and others. The primary consumers that live in the grasslands include prairie dogs, deer mice, jackrabbits, and grouse. Large grazing animals, such as deer, buffalo, and antelope, are abundant. These animals provide food for the predators: coyotes, bobcats, badgers, kit foxes, and others.

The *chaparral biome* is the most hospitable to people. The winter rainfall is low (about 15 to 20 inches, or 37.5 to 50 cm), and the summers are long, hot, and dry. This biome can be found in Southern California, around the Mediterranean coast, and on the southeastern tip of Australia.

This community is composed of mostly tall shrubs and dwarf trees: in California, mesquite, manzanita, California laurel, and small oak trees; and in Australia, eucalyptus trees and shrubs. The biome is often interspersed with grassland or shrub savanna.

Fire plays an important part in this biome. Many of the plants require the heat and scattering action of fire to induce germination. After a fire wildflowers and grasses spring up, encouraged by spring rains and the nutrient material released by fire from living vegetation.

The chaparral is home to the mule deer as well as wood rats, bobcats, cougars, brush rabbits, and mountain quail.

ECOSYSTEMS

All biomes are separated into various specialized communities (ecosystems) that form an interacting network of systems within the biotic community. Each individual ecosystem is a community within itself, containing many plant and animal species. Due to their specific adaptations, organisms within each ecosystem are much less tolerant to changing environmental conditions than the species of a broader, more generalized biome. An ecosystem is a smaller, specific biotic community containing several plant and animal species, all inhabiting a common space and interrelating with one another as well as with their physical environment.

All organisms within the ecosystem have their own specific *habitat*. For plants this is largely determined by the soil, light conditions, temperature, and moisture. Animals also depend upon these factors, but depend even more on the types of plants and other animals providing food and shelter.

As stated previously, the function an organism performs, or the job it does, is referred to as its niche. Some organisms may have many functions and thus fulfill a broad niche within the community. Other organisms fulfill specific functions and, thus, develop highly specialized niches. The hog-nose snake, for example, is specifically adapted to eat only toads. The garter snake, on the other hand, consumes a much wider variety of organisms and thus, has a broader, more general range.

FOOD WEBS

Most organisms fulfill their functions by performing their part in the food web, a general term used to describe the food relationships within the ecosystem. The food web is a way of transferring and transforming energy throughout the system. Since organisms may occupy one or more niches, these interrelationships resemble a web. All food relationships within a system begin with green plants, the *producers*. Plants form the base of the food web at the lowest energy level. Through the process of photosynthesis, they absorb sunlight, convert it to chemical energy, and then use this energy to produce glucose (a simple sugar). They store this glucose and convert it to fats, proteins, and carbohydrates.

Herbivores are the second energy level of the food web. These are animals that eat only vegetation, because they are capable of converting energy stored in plant tissue into animal tissue. The role of the herbivores, their niche, is essential to the survival of the ecosystem, for without them energy could not be transferred, and the other levels could not exist.

Herbivores are adaptable to a diet of cellulose. Specialized stomachs, teeth, and intestines allow these animals to ingest plant fiber, break it down, and convert it to usable energy for their bodies.

Carnivores, animals adapted to eat meat, form the third energy level of the food web. These animals are often larger and stronger than the herbivores they prey upon. They are the predators: animals that must kill in order to survive. There are many levels of carnivores. First-level carnivores feed directly upon herbivores, transforming this food source into their own animal protein. Second-level carnivores feed upon the first level. There may be higher levels of carnivores within an ecosystem, but the stored energy of the top level is eventually utilized by the *decomposers* when these larger animals die.

The word *omnivore* comes from *omni*, the Greek word meaning "all." Omnivores can be placed at all energy levels of the food web. The black bear feeds on small rodents, berries, and honey; it is a herbivore as well as a carnivore. The painted turtle feeds on vegetation, small fish, frogs, and dead fish. It feeds at all energy levels and also acts as a scavenger.

The *detritus* food web is the food web of the decomposers. It is often referred to as part of the nitrogen cycle. All living matter requires nitrogen, which is needed to build amino acids (proteins). Plants cannot fix or utilize nitrogen from the air but must obtain it through absorption from the soil, where bacteria convert it to usable form.

The ecosystem is an amalgam of species. It is the aggregation that gives the community its strength. Diversity within the ecosystem directly reflects the diversity of the physical environment. The more niches to fill, the more species to fill them. But diversity is also the key to survival for the ecosystem. Imagine a deciduous forest composed only of American elms. Along comes the Dutch elm beetle, and the ecosystem is destroyed.

Where a given organism exists within an ecosystem depends upon the *limiting factors* of the environment. All organisms possess limiting factors (extreme limits of the conditions under which they can survive). Plants and animals that cannot tolerate temperatures below the freezing level do not exist within the boreal forest. Desert plants do not develop in a rain forest. The limiting factors of an ecosystem greatly determine its *carrying capacity* (the number of organisms it can support).

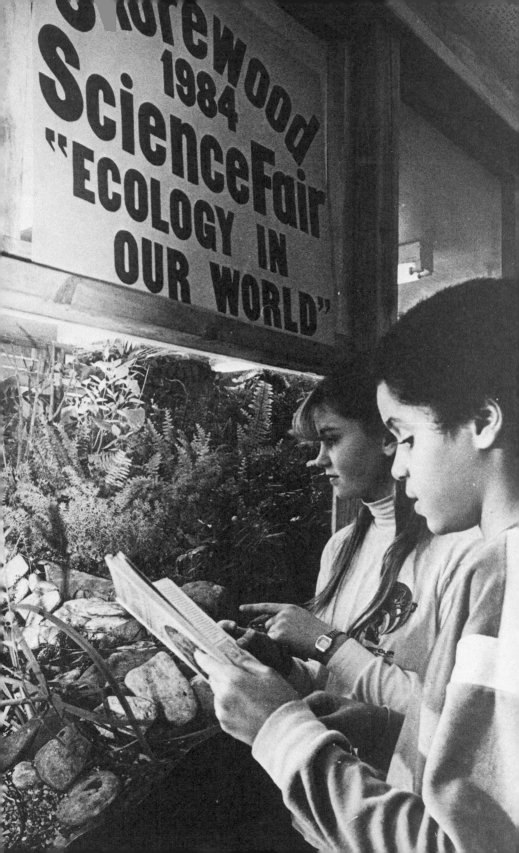

2

WHAT IS A
SCIENCE PROJECT?

A science project involves study of a problem or concept within any given scientific discipline. Ecology projects are based on environmental science and may also involve the fields of botany and zoology.

All science projects must have meaning to those performing them as well as to others. Projects must follow the scientific method of experiment and be research-oriented.

THE SCIENTIFIC METHOD

All projects begin with the *observation* of scientific phenomena. Observation is the key to a successful project. All other steps within the process of scientific research and discovery are based upon the disciplined observations of the scientist.

After observing an event, an ecologist or other scientist organizes the information that he or she has gathered. For example: Animals and plants are placed in their proper taxonomic categories; communities are placed within biomes and then into ecosystems; or the properties of organisms and their physical environments are defined and their interrelationships studied.

The observations of the scientific investigator should lead to a specific question or problem. This problem arises directly from observation and is called an *inference* or *prediction*. An educated guess as to the possible answer to the problem leads to the formulation of a *hypothesis*.

The hypothesis is the concept to be investigated. It is an inference or prediction that can be tested. It gives direction to scientific investigation. The investigator must always return to the basic premise in striving to prove or disprove the hypothesis. The experiment is based upon the hypothesis and relates directly to the problem. Your *results* will either confirm or refute your proposal. Your *conclusion* will state the validity of your projection. If the hypothesis is wrong, it should be restated and tested again.

As you move through the steps of scientific investigation, you will utilize a great many of the tools of science. Observations will be duly noted and recorded on tables of values, charts, or daily records. For example, you might keep a daily record on the requirements of plants for the process of photosynthesis.

By keeping the following log, you have a ready, documented source upon which to base your classifications, inferences, and predictions. As you follow the proper procedures of the scientific method of investigation, you will minimize error and move from proper investigation to conclusion. Valid conclusions should be drawn based on well-documented data only.

Data	Observations	Variables
9/28/83 (2nd week)	plant A (coleus) withered, droopy, and pale	no water
	plant B (coleus) pale, turgid, shows signs of disease	no light

plant C (coleus) lacks turgidity, pallid, and crisp	no CO_2
plant D (coleus-control), turgid, highly colored, upright, no signs of disease	full light, water, and CO_2

Ecological Research Projects:

Like any research project, an ecological project must be based upon sound scientific observation. Let's say you want to demonstrate the functioning of the photosynthetic equation and will attempt to interpret this process.

The project may begin with a simple statement of the photosynthetic equation; you might demonstrate that equation with a schematic diagram.

This done, you may choose to conduct several experiments on the photosynthetic process in order to prove that the equation really does function as stated. Three possible experiments are: Prove that plants contain chlorophyll and that chlorophyll does indeed absorb the radiant portion of the spectrum; prove that green plants release oxygen into the air as gas; or perhaps test for the Second Law of Thermodynamics.

You may decide to perform a project on plant senses. There are more plants than any other living organisms on Earth. Plants, like animals, are quite different from one another. Each species has its own characteristics and senses to ensure its survival. Plants sense moisture, light, touch, temperature, sounds, and chemicals.

All plants, especially perennials, operate on a light trigger. They have inherited traits that operate on a phototropic basis. You may want to develop a theory on the

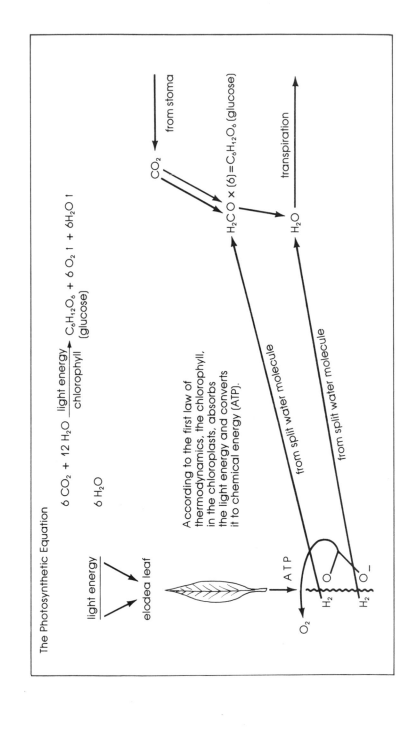

The Photosynthetic Equation

$$6 CO_2 + 12 H_2O \xrightarrow[\text{chlorophyll}]{\text{light energy}} C_6H_{12}O_6 + 6 O_2 \uparrow + 6H_2O \uparrow$$
$$\text{(glucose)}$$

$6 H_2O$

According to the first law of thermodynamics, the chlorophyll, in the chloroplasts, absorbs the light energy and converts it to chemical energy (ATP).

light energy

elodea leaf

ATP

O_2

H_2 O

H_2 O

from split water molecule

from split water molecule

CO_2

from stoma

$H_2CO \times (6) = C_6H_{12}O_6$ (glucose)

H_2O

transpiration

light trigger and the seasons. The project, of course, begins with observations of plants and their sensitivity to the number of hours of light per day. Note how plants change as the hours of daylight increase or decrease.

These observations duly recorded and classified, you may then develop a hypothesis based on the inferences drawn from the observations: If perennials indeed operate on a light trigger, then dormancy can be stayed by limiting the hours of light. The hypothesis is a testable statement. It is now up to you to test it and to record and analyze the results. Other problems will arise from the same photosynthetic reaction. Water requirements and carbon dioxide concentrations as variables in the experiment may also be explored.

HOW TO APPLY TO SCIENCE FAIRS

Most municipalities conduct their own science fairs, sponsored by the universities in the area. These institutions support science fairs in order to stimulate interest in science, as well as to encourage students to take up careers in science. The fairs also serve to uncover scientific ability in the participants.

Anyone interested in entrance requirements and eligibility may apply to the local university or check with the local library. Local newspapers have also sponsored gifted applicants to science fairs, especially local fairs. The awards at a science fair are determined by a rules committee and are usually given in the form of scholarships and trips.

All science fairs have their own rules and entry requirements. Those interested should obtain applications. Entry requirements are usually listed in an accompanying brochure. For international science fairs, write to

Science Service, Inc.
1719 N Street, N.W.
Washington, DC 20036

Environmental-awareness awards are given in order to promote environmental education and awareness. The government and environmental organizations sponsor these awards for worthy projects completed in the schools. For federal awards contact the local soil conservation district, usually located in the Federal Office Building. The federal Forest Service, which also sponsors some awards, is usually located in the Federal Office Building.

For local environmental awards go through the local city council or county board. Private awards are offered through foundations and national environmental organizations. Possibilities are the National Wildlife Federation, the Sierra Club, and local environmental associations for environmental education.

Apply to science fairs early, since space may be limited. You should also obtain a brochure or catalog listing the guidelines for entrance and space reservations.

IDENTIFYING AN ENVIRONMENTAL PROJECT

There are many projects to choose from when considering entrance into a science fair. Of course, the project should follow the rules of eligibility for the science fair. But nature is varied, and almost anything thought up by the human mind can become a science project. Because ecology is a general discipline, it encompasses all other scientific disciplines. Thus, you could enter with a chemistry-ecology or physics-ecology problem. The possibilities are limitless.

Ecological projects may be research-oriented, including experiments and demonstrations to prove a specific theory or observation. For example, Plant Senses—Water. What are the specific watering requirements of certain plants? How do plants obtain and retain water? This project requires a moisture-gradient box.

A moisture-gradient box is designed to demonstrate the water needs of plants. Set up on a 45-degree gradient, the box, when filled with water, creates a pond at the bottom. Water from this pond, through capillary action, works its way up the gradient. Plants at the bottom of the box will stand in water, plants in the middle will have moist soil, and plants at the top will be relatively dry.

Examples of three plant groups are sown. The plants are sown from the bottom of the box to the top: one row of hydrophytes (plants that need to be wet all the time), one row of mesophytes (plants that require a moderate amount of water), and one row of xerophytes (plants that require very little water). After the vegetation is in place, water is added until a pond is established at the bottom.

This is a controlled experiment, or an experiment in which the researcher controls the variables. You do not merely observe phenomena but *control* phenomena to test for hypothesized results. Most serious scientific research is accomplished by controlled experiments.

A log can be kept on the progress of the experiment. The pond is filled every day, but the plants themselves are not watered. The demonstration should be completed within two weeks. The results should be that the hydrophytes survived in the pond area, the mesophytes in the midsection, and the xerophytes at the top.

You could conclude from this demonstration that plants are definitely water-sensitive and specifically adapted to a given environment. Follow-up demonstrations could be done on plant roots and their hydrotrophic effect, exhibits of the various methods that plants use to store water could be created, and transpiration in plants could be studied.

HOW TO SET UP AND PRESENT
YOUR SCIENCE PROJECT

The United Nations has declared 1981 to 1990 to be the International Drinking Water Supply and Sanitation Decade, giving priority to the goal of bringing clean water to all the Earth's people. This goal is both admirable and practical, since water, both fresh and salt, is the medium for all life on Earth.

Experiments with water make good projects. Here are some characteristics of water, followed by appropriate projects.

Water provides dissolved minerals, gases, shelter, and food for the plants and animals that live in oceans, streams, creeks, ponds, and lakes. Water also carries minerals and salts for terrestrial organisms. Plants absorb minerals and dissolved salts through their root systems, while other organisms require water to move nutrients throughout their bodies.

Water is a compound composed of the elements hydrogen and oxygen (H_2O): two atoms of hydrogen to one atom of oxygen, bound together in a covalent bond.

The Physical Properties of Water:

Water heats up and cools down slowly, much more slowly than the atmosphere. The liquid stores large quantities of heat before its temperature begins to rise. This characteristic is referred to as *specific heat*. Due to their slow fluctuation in temperature, bodies of water tremendously affect their surroundings. For example, Lake Michigan influences the temperatures of the states of Wisconsin, Illinois, and Michigan.

A universal solvent, water dissolves almost any substance. This quality of water is important when considering its purity. The ability of water to dissolve most substances and the readiness with which other substances are attracted to it seem to guarantee its semipolluted state.

Projects on World Water:

All research projects begin with general observations (goals) that the researcher hopes to prove (achieve). Projects on water should start with the broadest generalization: to determine the workings and effects of the hydrologic cycle.

To determine how water becomes polluted, we must start with the givens that 1) all water moves about the planet Earth; 2) all the water within the biosphere is recycled. The Earth will never have any more or any less water than at present; all water within the biosphere is polluted. The goals of the researcher can be idealistic, such as to recognize the importance of water for our global well-being and to make an effort to improve the quality of human life worldwide by improving the quality of the world's water supply.

The researcher now moves from his or her observations toward classifying information or defining terms.

Surface Water: Water found on the surface of the Earth: lakes, rivers, streams, oceans.

Groundwater: Water found beneath the surface of the Earth: underground streams, wells.

Evaporation: Water from the surface of the Earth and from plants that escapes into the air as a gas.

Condensation: Water cooling into droplets.

Precipitation: Water falling in the form of rain, snow, sleet, hail.

After observations have been classified, inferences and predictions can be made. Since the quality of human life is directly related to and dependent upon the quality of the water supply, an understanding of the hydrologic cycle can lead to water-pollution abatement. This inference is based upon the pattern of human behavior throughout history. People learn from events that directly affect their lives.

Formulation of Hypothesis or Statement:
The quality of human life on Earth is directly related to the quality of the water within the hydrologic cycle.

Testing the Hypothesis

(setting up an experimental plan):

Materials (Parts One and Two):

> one large aquarium (fish tank) or other glass container (minimum 20 gallons)
> a glass or plastic divider, cut to fit the width of the above container (divider should be one-half the height of the tank)
> silicone sealant
> soil
> grass seed or some other type of small vegetation
> a glass cover, cut to fit on top of the tank
> alcohol burner
> open-top bell jar
> stopper for jar and plastic or rubber tubing
> tin dish
> ring stand
> sulfur
> paraffin wax
> tongs or clamps
> goldfish

Procedures (Part One):

The fish tank should be divided into sections. One-third will be a pond area, and two-thirds will be terrestrial. Place the glass divider in the tank one-third from one end. Use a silicone sealant to make it watertight. Run a bead of silicone along each side of the divider, where it meets the tank, and along the bottom edge. Allow the silicone to set for twenty-four hours.

When the divider is permanently in place, soil should be laid in the section behind it. This section covers two-thirds of the tank's area. Lay the soil an inch or two below the top of the divider, gradually inclining it at a 45-degree angle to the rear of the tank. This will eventually establish a moisture gradient for run-off.

The Hydrologic Cycle

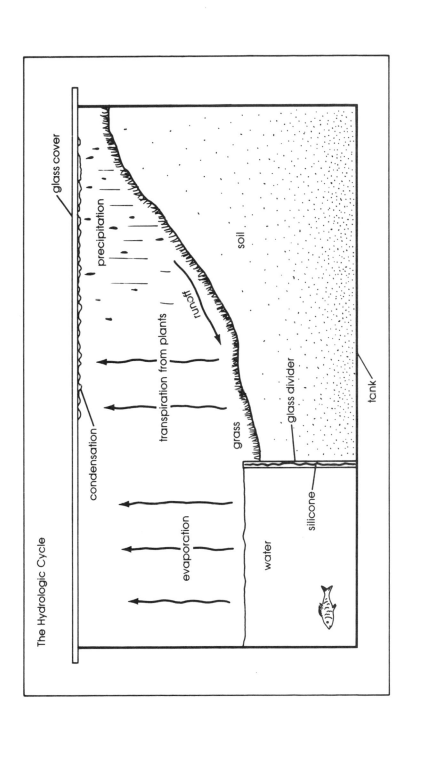

glass cover

precipitation

runoff

transpiration from plants

condensation

evaporation

soil

grass

glass divider

silicone

tank

water

Plant the grass seed or other vegetation, and allow time for it to germinate and establish its root systems. Water appropriately during this period (approximately two weeks). Do not overwater or fertilize. Overwatering will create mold and mildew, while fertilization will burn the roots.

Once the vegetation has established itself, set up the fish-pond section of the tank. Fill the remaining third of the tank with water. Go to the top of the glass divider but not over it. If you choose, you may put some minnows or a goldfish in the water.

Cover the tank with a glass plate, sealing it by wetting the rim of the tank. Your system is now enclosed, and the hydrologic cycle is in operation. Within several days the processes taking place should become visible. Water will evaporate from the pond and transpire from the vegetation. This gaseous water will cool on the glass plate and condense into droplets, which will precipitate back down to the pond and terrestrial sections of the system.

Analyzing Results and Observations (Part One):

This minisystem represents the hydrologic cycle within the biosphere. The water is locked in; there will never be any more or any less. It is constantly being recycled, traveling to all the different sections of the system. The system will work, and all will be fine as long as the water quality is satisfactory. But when the water becomes polluted, alterations occur within the system.

Observations: A record of what is actually observed must be kept.

Methods (Part Two): *Note:* *The fumes from the sulfur may be harmful. *Do not inhale.*
Acid Rain. Prepare the bell jar in advance. Close the opening with a stopper having a 2-foot (.6-m) rubber or

Acid Rain Demonstration

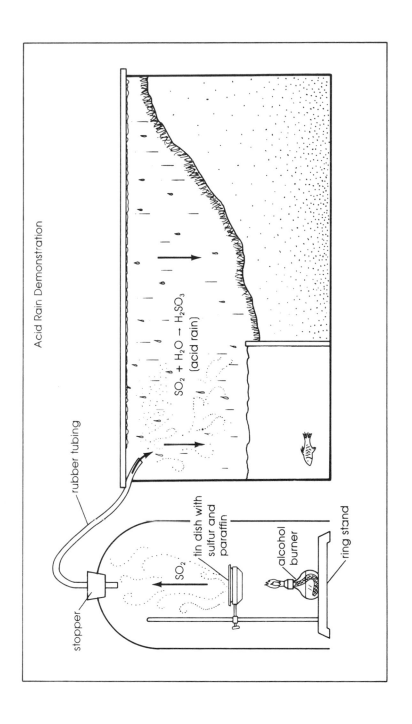

SO$_2$ + H$_2$O → H$_2$SO$_3$
(acid rain)

rubber tubing

stopper

SO$_2$

tin dish with
sulfur and
paraffin

alcohol
burner

ring stand

plastic tube extending from it. Place the end of the tube under the top of the minisystem just described.

When you have done this, put four measures of sulfur and several slivers of paraffin wax in a tin dish. Now set up a ring stand, placing the dish containing sulfur and paraffin on the ring and the alcohol burner beneath it. Ignite the alcohol burner. Heat the tin dish until the sulfur and wax melt and begin to generate sulfur dioxide (SO_2) gas. The gas will smoke. If the bell jar is large enough (preferable), set it over the smoking dish on the ring stand. If it is small, remove the smoking dish from the stand and place it under the jar. The tube will deliver the generated sulfur dioxide (SO_2) gas into the minisystem. The gas will combine with the water vapor to create sulfurous acid, or acid rain ($SO_2 + H_2O = H_2SO_3$).

Analyzing Results and
Observations (Part Two):
The researcher should test for acid with pH test paper. A slip of paper could be placed inside the system before generating the SO_2 gas.

The acid rain, over a period of time, will kill all the vegetation in the minisystem. Upon contact with the plants, the acid burns the living tissue. Acid dissolved into the soil is absorbed through the root hairs and, again, burns the living tissue.

Surface run-off will pollute the water in the pond and harm the vegetation and the fish. Eventually, as the tainted water circulates, the entire system will become polluted.

Conclusion:
The minisystem in this experiment is a hypothetical representation of the biosphere, which demonstrates how all systems within the biosphere are interrelated through the hydrologic cycle. Acid rain eventually impairs that community's water quality.

DEMONSTRATION OF THE SCIENCE PROJECT AT A SCIENCE FAIR

The researcher should identify the local and national fairs that are being conducted and then send for applications. After the forms are completed, contact the proper authorities: a teacher, school principal, counselor, or university professor.

The project should be identified properly and its relevance stated. Do this by listing observations and inferences, then stating the hypothesis. The rest is up to the science fair's applications committee.

Presentation at Fair

Two examples of your project should be set up and labeled. For example, in the above experiment, one working demonstration of the hydrologic cycle will be displayed. Also displayed will be an example of the long-term effects of the acid rain. If your project will show results without demonstrating the means, then only one display is necessary.

THE FORMAL REPORT

All science projects are more valuable when they are formally written up according to the standard practices of the academic discipline. There are usually seven steps in devising this report: observing, classifying, inferring, formulating a hypothesis, testing your hypothesis, analyzing results, and drawing conclusions. Your *observations* should be recorded and presented in a factual, objective manner. There is little room in science for subjective interpretation of phenomena. Once the basic *research* has been completed, all data must be *classified* and a specific problem identified and stated. This is an important step toward establishing the validity of your project. All scientists classify information. This lends order to the discipline and puts information in its proper perspective for further research or collection. The *inference* or *prediction* is based upon your research and stems from your classification of the data. These two abstractions are usually in the form of broad generalizations reflecting the basic problems or theories of your report. The inference and prediction are the final tools utilized before arriving at the *hypothesis*.

The hypothesis is usually a statement reflecting the behavioral characteristics of your problem. It is a projection of your thoughts that can be validated by *experimentation*. Therefore, the development of an experiment to test your hypothesis must be formulated and carried out. All *results* during your experiment refer back to the hypothesis. *Conclusions* are drawn from the experiment's results. After the experiment is concluded, your formal write-up will read like a recipe and allow other researchers to use your discoveries and methods. Further research may be suggested or indicated based upon the identification of a new problem arising from your experiment.

3

PROJECTS
ON AIR

The atmosphere is a mixture of gases that completely envelops the planet Earth and forms a major part of what is necessary for life to exist. This blanket of gases extends approximately 6 miles (9.654 km) up and is crowned by the ionosphere and the stratosphere.

The atmosphere, like water, is finite. All the air the biosphere is going to have is here right now. We will never have any more or any less. Because air is matter and has density, it may also become polluted. An amalgam of gases, air is everywhere. It fills every space available.

THE MAKEUP OF AIR

The gases in the air are nitrogen, 78 percent; oxygen, 21 percent; carbon dioxide, .02 percent; and argon and other rare gases, .08 percent.

As you can see, approximately 99 percent of the atmosphere consists of the two gases, nitrogen and oxygen, both of which are essential to life. Although nitrogen is vital for life processes, it is not easily converted to usable form. This gas is necessary for the formation of amino acids, which are found in all living things. Thus, transfer of nitrogen from the atmosphere to terrestrial organisms occurs throughout the nitrogen cycle.

Unlike nitrogen, oxygen, because it is a highly reactive gas, is assimilated by organisms quite readily. Oxygen is added to the atmosphere through the process of photosynthesis, while carbon dioxide, the other gas vital to life, is consumed during this process. Carbon dioxide is added to the atmosphere naturally through volcanic action and, today, via combustion from industry and transportation.

Air moves throughout the biosphere in two ways: wind and convection. Convection is the manner in which air rises and falls, according to temperature. Cold air, heavier than warm air, falls and, upon its descent, pushes the warmer, lighter air up. Due to convection, air pollution does not remain isolated or localized. It is only during a temperature inversion—a mass of air warmer than ground air moving over the surface—that convection is ineffective in filtering the air.

POLLUTANTS IN THE AIR

There are three basic types of air pollutants: gaseous, particulate, and aerosol. Atmospheric particulate pollution comes from many sources. A majority of the pollutants are natural. Natural forces put dust, aerosols, and particles in the air, where they are borne by the wind to all parts of the biosphere. Other particulate and aerosol pollutants originate from the activity of people. Industry, transportation, and construction are sources of this kind of air pollution.

There are four major gaseous pollutants of the atmosphere: sulfur-containing gases, carbon-containing gases, nitrogen-containing gases, and ozone. Only small amounts of these gases need be present to pollute the air. The presence of water vapor makes it possible for them to contaminate the air. Water vapor allows them to ionize and form the acid that is so corrosive.

Sulfur dioxide (SO_2) is a colorless, putrescent, heavier-than-air gas that rises in a cloud from volcanoes and industrial combustion of sulfur-bearing fuels. Hydrogen sulfide (H_2S), a gas generated from the decomposition of organic material, rises from bogs and swamps.

Carbon dioxide (CO_2) is a normal component of the atmosphere, but because of the massive combustion of fossil fuels in the last hundred years, many fear that the increase in the levels of this gas will upset the temperature balance within the biosphere.

Carbon monoxide (CO) enters the atmosphere through the incomplete combustion of fossil fuels. When it is inhaled, it combines with the hemoglobin of red blood cells and renders them ineffective.

Photochemical smog, a virulent vapor that covers a metropolitan area during a temperature inversion, is mainly composed of nitric oxide (NO) and nitrogen dioxide (NO_2). These oxides of nitrogen form from the combustion of gasoline at high temperatures. They combine with oxygen and, in the presence of sunlight, form their deadly compound. These products of combustion are known as peroxyacyl nitrates or, more commonly, PAN. They are the products of photochemical reactions in the air.

Ozone (O_3), an active form of oxygen, is a major gas of photochemical smog. It can be a strong pulmonary irritant when concentrated at terrestrial levels. When controlled, ozone has many productive uses. It is an excellent bacteriacide, especially in aquatic environments.

VOLCANIC POLLUTION OF THE AIR

A volcano is an opening in the Earth's crust connected to the mantle via a funnel or crater. Magma (hot, liquid rock), steam, and gases build in the crater and, when sufficient pressure has developed, explode through the skin of the Earth's surface in a violent eruption of particles, aerosols, and gases. The major gaseous pollutant produced by a volcano is sulfur dioxide (SO_2). The eruption also expels billions of particles into the air. Many of these particulates stay aloft for years, while others settle to the surface.

Problem: Volcanoes seem to invest the air with foreign matter. What type of material is this matter? Is it poisonous? How does it pollute?

Materials for the Project:
   plaster of Paris
   screening
   wood (some pieces for framing and a large slab
      for a platform)
   paint
   tin can
   ammonium dichromate
   paraffin wax
   sulfur
   wooden kitchen matches
   lead-acetate test paper
   filter paper
   razor blade
   scissors
   tweezers
   tin dishes
   mortar and pestle
   beaker
   water

THIS EXPERIMENT SHOULD BE PERFORMED UNDER THE SUPERVISION OF AN ADULT. IT MUST BE CONDUCTED IN AN AREA WITH PROPER VENTILATION—AN EXHAUST FAN IS PREFERABLE.

Hypothesis: If volcanoes expel foreign matter into the air, then they must pollute the air.

Methods for the Project:
The frame of the volcanic mountain will be constructed

from screening and plaster of Paris. Its design should be similar to existing volcanoes, Mount St. Helens, for instance. The crater, the tin can, is to be at the top, with the cone of the mountain molded to cover its surface. The model, when dry, should be painted to your liking.

Break off approximately 200 matchheads and place them inside a safe container. Combine 30 teaspoons of ammonium dichromate with 10 teaspoons of sulfur and 4 teaspoons of paraffin wax shavings. Grind the mixture together.*

Layer your mixture and matchheads in the crater of the volcano until you fill the cone. The layers should be thin to allow the matchheads to ignite the mixture at each successive level. Start at the bottom of the cone with a layer of matchheads, and then spoon in the mixture.

Light the top layer of matchheads, and the volcano will begin to erupt. Particles and aerosols will explode into the air, and a greenish lava will ooze down the sides of the mountain. Billows of smoke filled with sulfur dioxide gas will rise from the crater.

Test for sulfur dioxide by wetting a strip of lead-acetate test paper and holding it over the crater with a pair of tweezers. This paper turns gray to brownish black in the presence of sulfur dioxide. You may also rig some filter paper over the crater to capture the particulate matter being emitted.

Presentation at Fair:

You should have two volcanoes: one as a model and the other functional. Accompanying your formal report should be strips of tested lead-acetate paper and filter paper. You may also have samples of real volcanic dust (perhaps from Mount St. Helens), as well as dust from your mock volcano. An extra might be a diagrammed display of how

---

*WEAR A MASK WHILE WORKING WITH THIS MIXTURE.

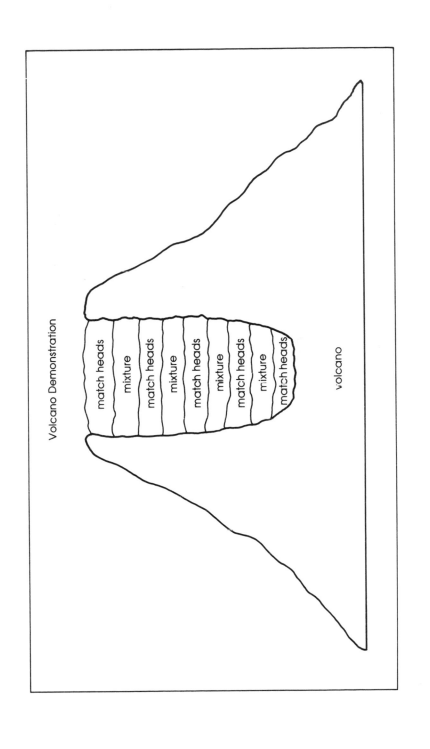

Volcano Demonstration

match heads

mixture

match heads

mixture

match heads

mixture

match heads

mixture

match heads

volcano

volcanoes are formed and the role they have played in shaping our planet.

FOREST FIRES AND THEIR ROLE
IN NATURALLY POLLUTING THE AIR

Many natural phenomena pollute the air. Forest fires, which are a cyclical natural happening, pollute the atmosphere in much the same manner as do volcanoes. They emit carbon dioxide and carbon monoxide. They also project tons of particle debris, in the form of ash, soot, and cinders, into the atmosphere.

Problem: How do forest fires pollute the air?

Materials for the Project:
    a large fish tank (minimum 10-gallon)
    gravel or sand (enough to cover bottom of tank
        2 inches (5 cm) deep)
    a box of wooden kitchen matches
    filter paper
    glass cover for fish tank
    tape
    paper straw
    small jar filled with water

Hypothesis: If forest fires cause air pollution, then particulates and gases will accumulate during the laboratory simulation.

Methods for the Project:
Fill the bottom of the fish tank with 2 inches (5 cm) of sand or gravel. Place approximately 25 to 30 matches in a tight circle in the center of the tank. Tape a piece of filter paper to the glass cover (tape should be off to the side so it will not burn). Wet the rim of the fish tank so that the glass will form a seal over the tank. The straw is going to be

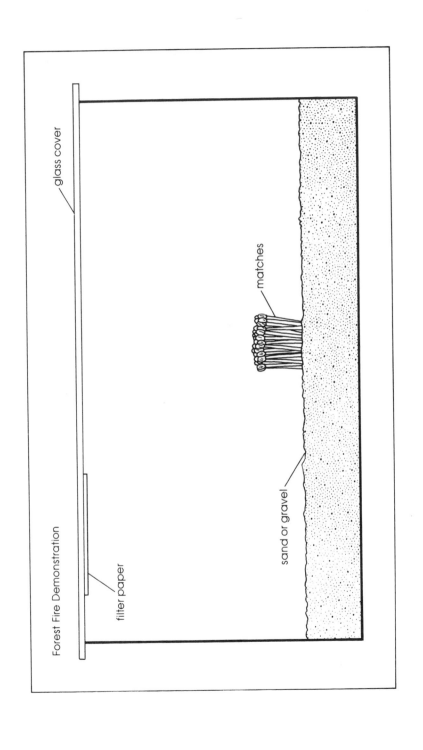

Forest Fire Demonstration

glass cover

filter paper

matches

sand or gravel

used to ignite the matches in the tank. Light the straw first. Then light the matches in the tank with the lit straw and immediately slide the glass cover over the top.

The matches will ignite and send billows of smoke, ash, and soot into the air. The filter paper will collect the aerosols and particulates. Carbon soot will form on the glass cover, and ash will litter the bottom of the tank.*

Presentation at Fair:

This project can be demonstrated in the same manner as the volcano. It might also be a good idea to show both this and the previous project together as major sources of natural air pollution.

AUTOMOBILE EMISSIONS AND PARTICULATES IN THE AIR

Air pollution has been and continues to be a major environmental problem in urban industrial societies. Some physicians and respiratory experts believe it is one of our most pressing problems. This polluted atmosphere directly affects and threatens the health, and even the lives, of people in our major population centers.

Particulate matter in the air has caused environmental problems throughout history. Dust and smoke became a major problem with the onset of the Industrial Revolution and the addition to the atmosphere of the by-products resulting from the combustion of coal. Today air pollution problems are compounded by the by-products of the gasoline internal combustion engine, oil-burning factories,

*CARBOXYHEMOGLOBIN. BE CAREFUL WHEN YOU CONDUCT THIS EXPERIMENT. IT PRODUCES CARBON MONOXIDE GAS, WHICH COMBINES WITH HEMOGLOBIN IN THE RED BLOOD CELLS FAR MORE READILY THAN OXYGEN. THE MOLECULE FORMED, CARBOXYHEMOGLOBIN, PREVENTS THE HEMOGLOBIN FROM CARRYING OXYGEN TO THE BODY'S CELLS.

and radioactive dusts emitted by nuclear explosions over the past forty years.

The air is continually being bombarded by foreign particles that are the by-products of human civilization. Particles from industry are ever present in urban environments; for example, fine dust from cement factories and chemicals from breweries, steel mills, and foundries. Today we are adding foreign particles to the air faster than we can determine their effects on the environment.

In order to understand how particulate matter, smoke, and dust can pollute the air, we must first understand the basic properties of the atmosphere: Air is matter; it has weight and takes up space.

Problem: To prove that air is matter.

Materials for the First Experiments in the Project:
   a long dowel or yardstick
   three strings, cut into 12-inch (30-cm) lengths
   two balloons
   two flasks
   one single-hole stopper
   two funnels
   a sharp pin or probe
   a beaker filled with water

Methods for the Project:
Blow the two balloons up to exactly the same size, tying their ends so no air escapes. With the two pieces of string, tie one balloon to each end of the dowel. This done, tie the third piece of string to the center of the dowel with a loose knot (the string in the center must be adjustable from side to side). Balance the balloons by adjusting the center string. Now use the sharp pin to puncture one of the balloons.

The end of the dowel with the unpopped balloon will dip toward the floor, proving that air has weight.

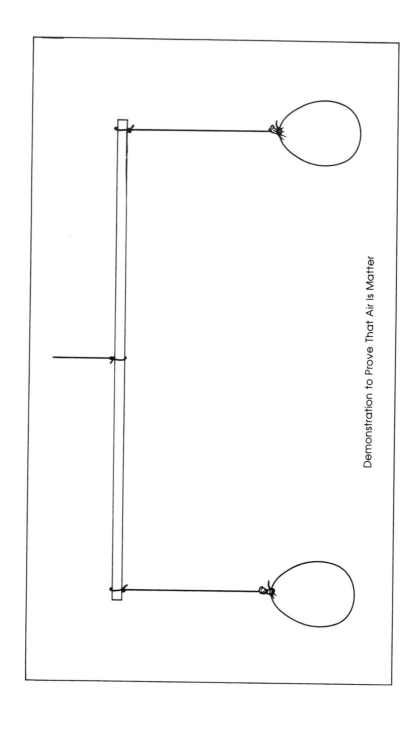

Demonstration to Prove That Air Is Matter

Place one funnel in an empty flask and a second funnel through the one-hole stopper into the other empty flask. (Glycerine can be used as a lubricant so as to slip the funnel into the stopper easily.) Pour water from the beaker into the funnel without the stopper. The water will run through the funnel and into the flask.

Pour water into the other funnel. The water will not run through the funnel but will fill up the cup. This demonstrates that air takes up space. Air can escape from the flask without the stopper and allow the water to replace it. Air cannot escape from the flask with the stopper. The water cannot enter this flask because the flask already contains air.

Air has weight and takes up space. Air is matter. All matter has density (a thickness of consistency). Since air has density, it can absorb gases and support particulate matter.

Presentation of These
Two Experiments
as Part of Project:

Have two sets of dowels and balloons. Attach one set to a bulletin board or divider in your booth. This example should show what the experiment looks like when it is completed. The dowel should be attached at an angle with the filled balloon at the lower end. A written description of the experiment should accompany these results. The other set of balloons and dowel should demonstrate the experiment.

On a table below the balloon demonstration should be your flask and funnel experiment. Again have two sets of equipment. One should show the results of your experiment. The other should be ready for demonstration. A written explanation should also accompany this experiment.

Problem: How do particulate wastes from the transportation industry pollute the air?

Demonstration to Prove That Air Takes Up Space

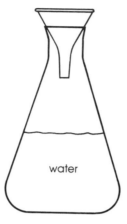

water

flask without stopper
Water goes through
and fills flask.

water

flask with stopper
Water stays in cup
of funnel.

Materials for the Project:
   filter paper
   six 3- x 5-inch index cards
   opaque microscope or magnifying glass
   several automobiles or trucks

Hypothesis: If transportation puts particulate matter in the atmosphere, then this particulate matter will be measurable in the laboratory.

Methods for the Project:
Prepare the six index cards to test automobiles for particulate emissions. Find six people who are willing to have their automobiles tested. Have them start their cars and allow them to warm up for about a minute. Now hold an index card approximately 6 inches (15 cm) from the automobile exhaust pipe for about one minute.*

After collecting the particles, bring them back to the laboratory and place them on a microscope, or look at the cards under a magnifying glass. Compare the particles on the filter paper to the chart on page 44. Write the approximate number of particles per square inch on the card. Make up six more cards to be set up for industries.

Locate six different factories and ask permission to place the cards on a window of a home or business nearby. Leave the cards in place for about one week. Collect the cards and take them back to the laboratory. Place these cards under the microscope and compare them to the chart above. Write the approximate number of particles per square inch on the card.

Presentation at Fair:
This project should be presented along with the previous two experiments proving that air is matter. The tested

*CAUTION. AVOID INHALING FUMES.

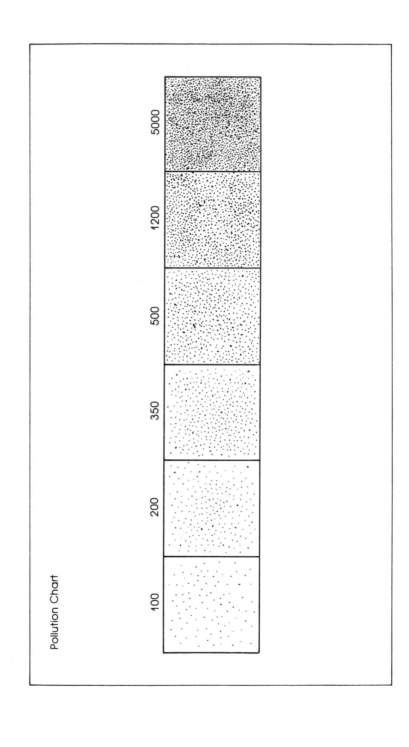

Pollution Chart

100   200   350   500   1200   5000

index cards should be displayed on a bulletin board. Two more sets, one from an automobile and the other from an industry, should be placed under a microscope on a table. The chart showing the number of particles per square inch should be close by for comparison. A written description of the experiment should accompany the display.

It might be a good idea to display photographs of air pollution from industry and transportation. You may also wish to explain what chemicals accompany this type of air pollution.

AUTO EMISSIONS, CONVECTION, TEMPERATURE INVERSIONS, AND PHOTOCHEMICAL SMOG

Every inhabitant of a major metropolitan area knows the problems of air pollution. All have experienced ozone alerts and the burning, itching eyes caused by photochemical smog.

The major contributor to photochemical smog is transportation (60 percent), due to the internal combustion engine. This engine does not burn gasoline completely. Complete combustion would result in the release into the atmosphere of carbon dioxide (CO_2), heat, and water vapor, none of which are toxic air pollutants.

Incomplete combustion of gasoline at high temperatures results in the formation of several poisons, which enter the atmosphere, react with the ultraviolet light from the sun, and form the deadly compounds that comprise photochemical smog: PAN (the oxides of nitrogen, nitric oxide (NO), nitrogen dioxide (NO_2); carbon monoxide (CO); and ozone (O_3)).

Problem: How do temperature inversions trap pollutants and create photochemical smog?

Materials for the Project:
    a large shoe box
    plastic wrap
    two cardboard tubes
    candle
    long match
    paper towels
    aluminum foil
    two bell jars, each with a hole in the top
    three stoppers and delivery tubes
    large jar
    3- x 5-inch index cards
    petroleum jelly
    alcohol or Bunsen burner
    flasks
    heat lamp on stand
    scissors
    tape
    clay
    ice cubes
    water
    air pump
    ring stand

Hypothesis: If a temperature inversion traps pollutants, then photochemical smog will result.

Methods for the Project:
This project is a demonstration of how three different processes can lead to photochemical smog. The presenter should use a divided-type backing at the fair with research on photochemical smog displayed in charts and pictures. Data on automobile emissions, industrial output, and weather would be appropriate.

A temperature inversion occurs when a mass of warm air moves over stagnant, cooler, surface air. This warm air mass traps the surface air and forms a seal over the area, enclosing all of the toxins that are produced by modern society.

Cut the front portion out of a shoe box (or any large box with a lid), and cover the opening with clear plastic wrap. Tape the plastic wrap to the front of the box, forming an airtight seal.

Cut two holes in the top of the box (one at each end), just large enough for two paper towel tubes. Push the tubes into the holes and seal the openings with tape in order to ensure an airtight seal.

Set a candle in a clay base under one of the chimneys, and then tape the top of the box in place. The candle should be at least 2 inches (5 cm) lower than the chimney.

Use a long match, and light the candle by putting it into the chimney.* (The box is sealed, and this is the only way to light the candle.) Once the candle is lit, allow the box to warm for approximately five minutes.

Light an alcohol or Bunsen burner, and hold a tightly wrapped piece of industrial paper toweling or a stick of wood into the flame. After the paper or wood catches fire, allow it to burn for a short while, and then blow it out. It should smoke profusely. Now hold the smoking paper over the chimney without the candle.

The cold (heavier) air above the smoking paper will push the smoke down through the chimney. The smoke will then warm, rise toward the candle, and exit the convection box via the opposite chimney.

Convection currents and wind purify air. These two natural forces move polluted air rising from industrial centers and dilute them in an ocean of pure air. A temperature inversion prevents normal convection. The warmer air mass moves over the cooler ground air and traps it.

Fill a large jar or deep tank with cold water and ice cubes.

*CAUTION. BE CAREFUL WHILE LIGHTING CANDLE.

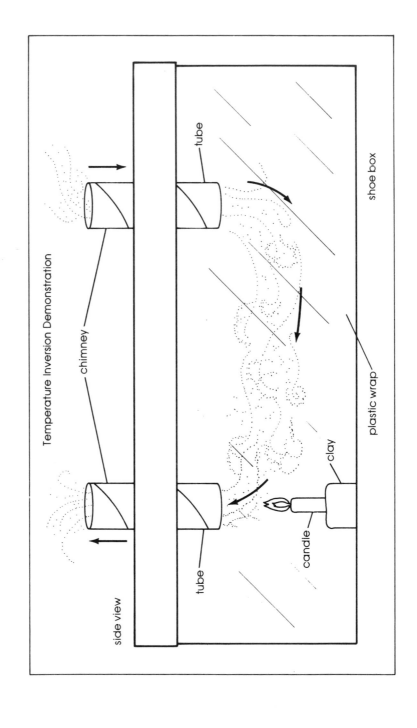

Temperature Inversion Demonstration

side view

chimney

tube

tube

candle

clay

plastic wrap

shoe box

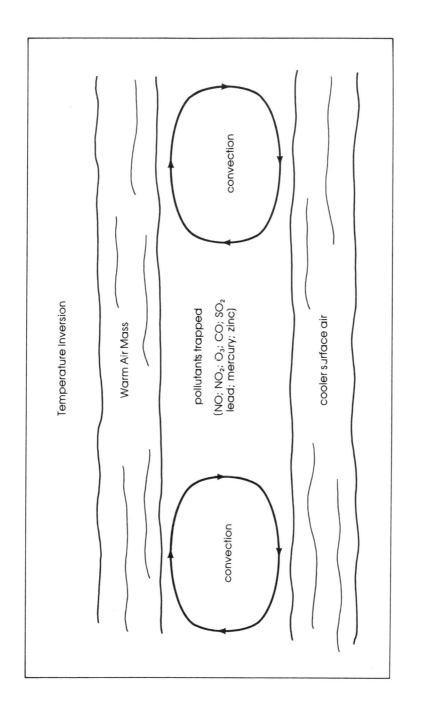

Temperature Inversion

Warm Air Mass

pollutants trapped

(NO; NO_2; O_3; CO; SO_2
lead; mercury; zinc)

convection

convection

cooler surface air

Set a heat lamp or powerful light over the mouth of the jar and allow the air in this area to warm, creating a temperature inversion.

Create a gas generator by filling a 500-ml flask with ten measures of sulfur and one measure of paraffin slivers. Place a two-hole stopper in the flask, with plastic tubing coming out of each hole. (One tube should be 36 inches (90 cm) and the other 15 inches (37.5 cm).) Attach the 15-inch (37.5-cm) plastic tube to an air pump, and extend the other tube to the inside of the jar. Heat the flask until the mixture of sulfur and paraffin melts and creates sulfur dioxide gas. Once the flask is filled with the yellow vapor, remove the heat source and switch on the air pump. The gas will be transferred from the flask to the jar.

Allow the gas to fill the jar and then switch off the air pump. The gas will now be trapped in the temperature inversion. Convection will take place in the jar, but the gas will not be able to rise through the warm air at the mouth of the jar.

Presentation at Fair:
Have all three experiments set up and ready to demonstrate on an hourly schedule. If you like, you may have visual examples of what the temperature inversion does to cities, such as Los Angeles or New York. You should also have the formal report written up and displayed for spectators to read.

OTHER PROJECTS ON AIR

1. Do a study on changing weather conditions based on the inference that recent volcanic action cools the Earth. Collect data on volcanic emissions and research their effect on the atmosphere and especially on the stratosphere. Diagram weather patterns and demonstrate the effects of the jet streams on weather.

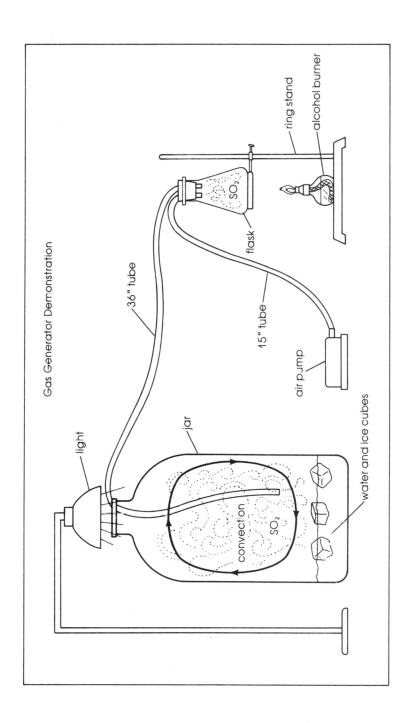

Gas Generator Demonstration

light

36" tube

jar

convection

SO₂

water and ice cubes

15" tube

air pump

flask

SO₂

ring stand

alcohol burner

2. Another project can be presented on the effects of carbon dioxide (CO_2) and changing weather conditions on Earth. Base your study on the premise that increased amounts of CO_2 in the atmosphere will raise the temperature of the planet. Show the effects of this gas on rain by doing pH tests on rainwater exposed to CO_2 and rainwater not exposed. How does CO_2 affect photosynthesis? Demonstrate by a controlled experiment with plants. Expose some plants to excessive amounts of CO_2 and others to normal amounts. Measure the results by testing for sugar (Benedick's solution) and starch (iodine).

4

PROJECTS
ON WATER

Plants, like animals, are adapted to their own specific environments. They are specialized to live within a given ecosystem, where they fulfill their biological function by filling a given niche. Plants are adapted not only to measured amounts of water but also to the amount of sunlight they receive, the condition of soil they sink their roots into, and the atmospheric conditions that surround them. Some plants grow only in water, some grow only in bogs, and others grow only in shade. The varieties are unlimited and give the curious mind many ideas for future science projects.

A MOISTURE-GRADIENT BOX

A moisture-gradient box is designed to demonstrate how certain plants are adapted to specific water conditions. Three types of plants will be studied: wet (hydrophytes), dry (xerophytes), and moderate (mesophytes). Each of these plants require a different amount of water.

Problem: How are different types of plants adapted to varying water conditions?

Materials for the Project:
    a large wooden box (3 feet x 5 feet x 1 foot)

(.9m x 1.5m x .3m). The box should be water-proof and watertight (either fiberglassed or lined with a plastic-type material).

soil

gravel

hydrophyte (elodea, myrophyllum, pickerel-weed)

xerophyte (cactus or succulent)

mesophyte (bean, petunia)

several 2 x 4s

water

Hypothesis: If plants are adapted to specific water conditions, then xerophytes, hydrophytes, and mesophytes will survive only in those conditions to which they are adapted.

Methods for the Project:
The moisture-gradient box should be set up at a 45-degree gradient. This is accomplished by using the 2 x 4s for support. (A simpler box at home can be leaned against a stack of books.)

After the box is set up on the gradient, the gravel and soil can be put inside. The bottom of the box should have a thin layer of gravel for drainage. Soil should cover the entire area to three-quarters of the depth of the box.

When the soil is ready, three rows of vegetation should be planted. In the middle should be the meso-phytes, flanked by xerophytes and hydrophytes.

Pour water into the lower section of the box and keep adding water until a small pond or puddle forms. Allow the water to be absorbed by the soil, and then add more. Do this until no more water is absorbed. Do not water the plants. Just fill bottom of box.

Keep a daily log on the vegetation in the moisture-gradient box. Expect results within one week to ten days.

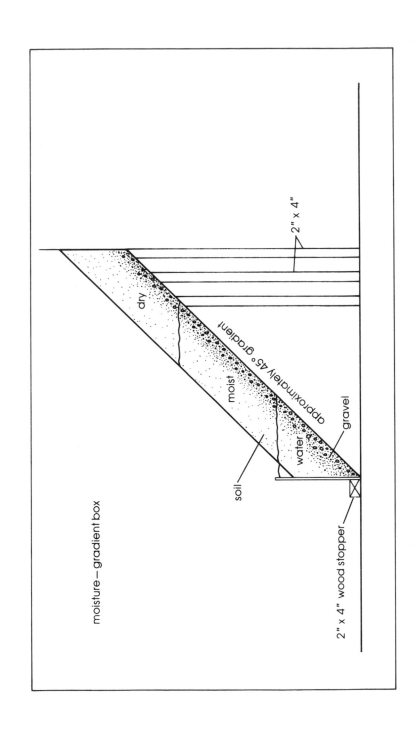

moisture—gradient box

dry

moist

water

gravel

soil

approximately 45° gradient

2" x 4"

2" x 4" wood stopper

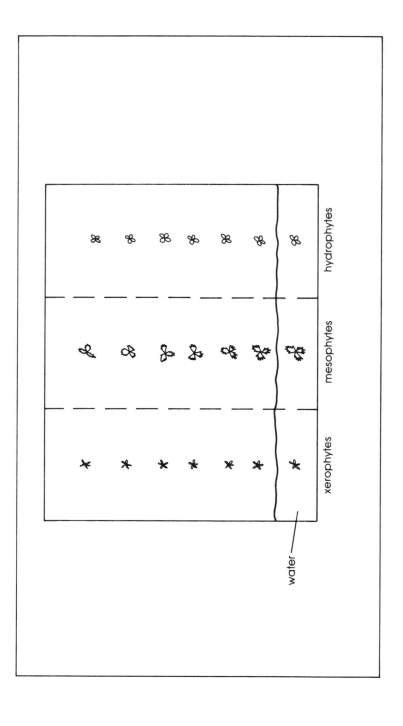

Presentation at Fair:

The presenter should have two moisture-gradient boxes established. One should demonstrate the procedure followed in the project, and the other should show the results. The researcher's log should be displayed, showing his or her interpretation of the data and a listing of the variables.

SUCCESSION

There are very few things, if any, within the biosphere that escape change. Some of these changes are instantaneous, others slower, and others take place so slowly that one cannot see them occurring. Change is a constant in a biosphere that is capricious. *Succession* is the term used by naturalists to describe the orderly and progressive replacement of one community (biome or ecosystem) by another until a stable community occupies the area.

The development of a small lake or pond into a forest occurs over many thousands of years and goes through many *pioneer stages*. A pioneer stage is characterized by the plants and animals present in the temporary community on the road toward the climax, or stable, community for any given region.

The beginning of any successive order is the pioneer community. In a pond or lake this is characterized by a bottom devoid of vegetation. Yet from its inception, succession occurs. The first stages are the influx of colonies of animal and plant plankton (zooplankton and phytoplankton). These microscopic forms of life complete their cycles, die, and settle at the bottom of the lake, forming a layer of decomposing material.

Accompanying the stages of plankton and directly dependent upon them are other forms of life: pumpkinseed sunfish, bluegills, largemouth bass, crappies, and northern pike. There are also caddis flies, fairy shrimp, water fleas, and other aquatic insects.

As the decaying materials at the bottom of the lake deepen, they create a layer of nutrient-rich material that serves as a bed for other aquatic organisms (elodea, pondweed, and branching green algae). This strata of aquatic vegetation occurs at the edges and in the shallow regions of the pond and eventually fills in the entire lake.

As the lake becomes more shallow, the areas along the shoreline fill with pioneer plants of the terrestrial ecosystem, and the succession from a pond to a forest becomes visible. Eventually, organic and inorganic sediment builds up on the bottom of the lake, and the lake ecosystem itself will change. The organisms that required a hard, rock-bottom lake (smallmouth bass) will vanish, to be replaced by life forms that prefer muck.

Over a period of time the lake will shallow up and become a marsh or a bog. The organic structure will change since the species that inhabit these wet areas are very different from those that inhabit a lake. The sediment deposit continues and rises above the water level to create a meadow; the meadow is overtaken by shrubs; the shrubs eventually give way to the climax forest.

Problem: How does succession occur in a lake?

Materials for the Project:

> four large fish tanks (minimum 50-gallon)
> aerators for water
> filters for water
> gravel
> soil (marsh) and grasses
> soil (woodland)
> variety of plant life for pond, wetlands
> screen for top of tanks
> light for over tanks
> screening to mold bottom of pond

fiberglass cloth and resin to make bottom of
    pond
small pieces of wood
brown paint
rocks
sand
paintbrushes
silicone caulk and caulking gun
fish (variety)
tadpoles
frogs (leopard)
crayfish
newts
salamanders
worms
garter snake

Methods for the Project:
Establish four tanks representing the four stages of succession in lakes. The *first stage* should depict a lake in its early phases.

Mold screening in a 50- to 60-gallon fish tank to reflect the basin and edge of a pond. Support the screening (if necessary) with small pieces of wood. Cover the screening with fiberglass cloth and resin (follow directions on the label of the resin can). The sides of the pond should be steep, the pond deep.

Place an underground filter at the bottom of the tank. This will keep the water clean. The bottom of the pond should be covered with gravel and rocks. The sides, which are the terrestrial sections, should be covered with a marshy soil. Fill the tank with water and let it stand for several days before introducing any organisms.

Organisms introduced in the early stages of a pond should be those that prefer deep, clear, cool water and a hard bottom. The vegetation should be the floating variety. A few elodea may be planted at the edges, but, for

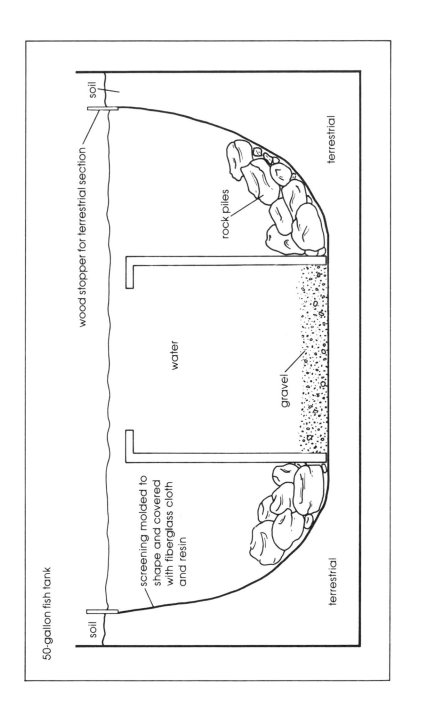

50-gallon fish tank

soil

wood stopper for terrestrial section

soil

terrestrial

rock piles

water

gravel

terrestrial

screening molded to shape and covered with fiberglass cloth and resin

the most part, the aquatic vegetation will be floating, nonrooted plants.

Aquatic animal life should consist of crayfish, perch, rock bass, and, if possible, a smallmouth bass.* Several minnows may be introduced to feed the perch and bass. Some marsh grass or other low-growing marsh plants may be planted in the terrestrial section.

The *second stage* in the successional process depicts a mature lake or pond and reflects the differences in structure and organisms. Mold screening (in the same manner as before) to simulate the basin and edges of a mature lake or pond. A power-flow filter should be used to clean the tank, and an aerator, to oxygenate the water. The fiberglass sides should be painted brown to simulate the silt built up over the years.

Rocks and gravel may be glued to the fiberglass to look like a mature lake. The bottom is a mixture of silt, gravel, and muck. Aquatic plants have established themselves and rooted near the edges of the pond. The surface area for water has decreased slightly, demonstrating how the forest has crept closer, and the aquatic organisms are changed to mirror those that exist within a mature pond.

The *third stage* in the succession simulates an aged pond or lake. Mold two layers of screening and fiberglass, one to show the original bottom of the pond and the other to demonstrate the results of succession.

Again the fiberglass should be painted and made to simulate the sides of an aging pond. The pond bottom should contain decayed matter, reflecting the silting over the years. Aquatic plants are well established, and animal life has changed.

The *final stage* of the pond's successional process is demonstrated by molding three layers of fiberglass, the first showing the original gravel bottom of the pond. The

*TO KEEP AND DISPLAY GAME FISH, A SPECIAL LICENSE IS REQUIRED.

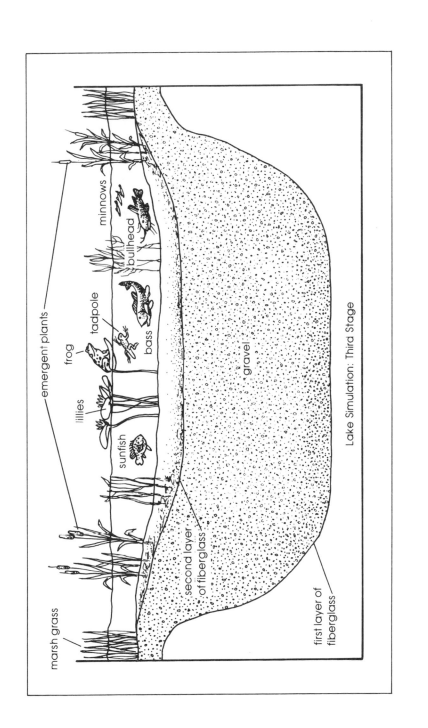

marsh grass

emergent plants

lillies

frog

tadpole

sunfish

bass

bullhead

minnows

second layer
of fiberglass

first layer of
fiberglass

gravel

Lake Simulation: Third Stage

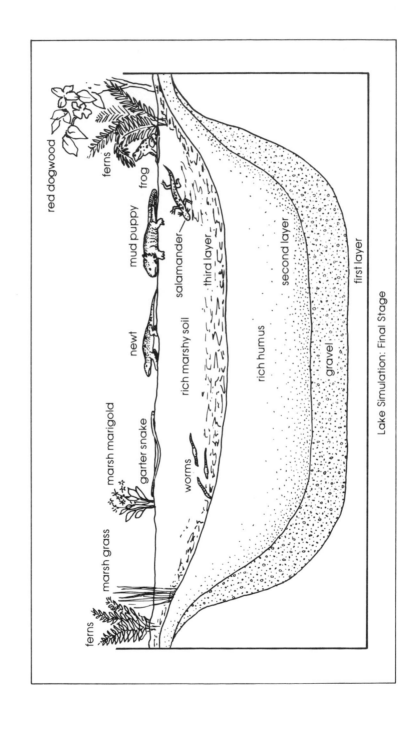

red dogwood

ferns

frog

mud puppy

salamander

third layer

second layer

first layer

rich humus

gravel

newt

rich marshy soil

marsh marigold

garter snake

worms

marsh grass

ferns

Lake Simulation: Final Stage

second layer will include the rich layer of organic humus created by the silting over the years. The third layer, a marshy, grassy area, is on its way toward a climax terrestrial ecosystem.

Presentation at Fair:
Present this project by displaying the four stages of succession with a written explanation of each. Also, photographs of actual successional stages would be helpful to viewers of the exhibit. Labeled diagrams of each stage should be displayed next to the models.

RIVER ECOSYSTEMS

All rivers and streams are formed by the hydrologic cycle and follow paths of the least resistance back to their original source, the sea. Sources, or origins, of streams on land begin as run-offs from glaciers in the mountains, as outlets from ponds or lakes, or they may arise from springs, marshes, and confluences of creeks. Streams and rivers are characterized by running water and, depending on the current and depth, influence the lives of the organisms inhabiting this flowing ecosystem.

In streams and rivers the movement of water makes the life-supporting conditions quite different from those in lakes and oceans. Since sunlight penetrates water, except in the deepest and muddiest rivers, photosynthesis may occur at all levels. Also, because of the movement of the water, there is little variation in temperature from bottom to top.

Life in streams and rivers varies not from the bottom to the top, but along its length. The variance of habitat depends upon the swiftness of current rather than the depth of the water.

A swift-running river is usually shallow and strewn with rocks. As the river swirls and ripples along its path, the organisms in this environment must be able to withstand the tearing force of the current. Plants are most abundant among the bubbling rapids, as they cling to the rocks, forming a slippery green surface just under the water. These are the hardy producers of the river's ecosystem.

The rocks of the riverbed provide a variety of habitats for a broad spectrum of life. The side of a rock facing the current receives the full brunt of the force of the moving water. Only the hardiest of organisms live and grow there. The downstream side of that same rock is protected from the full force of the current. Here a form of plant life may grow that is more delicate than its neighbor on the other side of that same rock.

Beneath the rocks and in the crevices between them live a wide variety of animals. Many are the larva or pupa of such insects as caddis flies, stoneflies, and mayflies. As they cling to the rocks with their claws, the swift-moving current supplies them with oxygen and food.

Most life in swift-moving streams lives in the riffles, but a good many live in the pools of the stream. Many animals that exist in the riffles are moved by the current to the pools. If they remain in the pool, the majority of these animals will die of suffocation. This is not because the pool of water does not have enough oxygen to support life. It does. Animals that inhabit the riffles have low-quality respiratory systems. Because of the relative stillness of the water in the pools, their bodies become covered with substances that prevent them from taking in enough oxygen.

In the deeper water of the pools, sediments and organic debris settle to the bottom. Here insects and other organisms that cannot withstand the swift current make their homes. The decomposer organisms live at the bottom of the pool and convert organic debris into nutrients. Most trout, for example, rest in pools but enter the riffles to feed.

As the current slows and a stream deepens, a noticeable change occurs in the habitat of the water. Sediments and decaying organic debris settle to the bottom and accumulate. The river bottom becomes covered with mud and other sediments. The color of the water is brownish, and the river absorbs much more heat from the sun. Warmer water holds less oxygen than fast-moving streams.

Organisms of the fast-moving stream are replaced by organisms of the slower, deeper water. Brook trout give way to largemouth bass and northern pike, minnows, and crayfish. Plant life is anchored by roots to the bottom of the river and is usually abundant along the banks. Plankton develop, and such insects as water striders and dragonflies are plentiful on the water's surface.

As the river slows and the water continues to get deeper, more silt is built up along the bottom, and the decomposers increase. Rooted vegetation increases, and bottom feeders, such as bullheads, catfish, and carp, become prevalent. Duckweed floats on these quiet backwaters and lies over the water's surface, touching emergent plants, such as cattails, arrowheads, and water lilies. Here the river becomes much more like a eutrophic lake, a lake that is aging prematurely.

Various forms of green algae float in the slow-moving streams, as backswimmers, water boatmen, and diving beetles swim on the water's surface. Zooplankton eat the algae and are, in turn, eaten by minnows (golden shiners, blacknose dace, northern fatheads). Largemouth bass and northern pike prey upon the minnows, while crayfish, bacteria, fungi, and certain worms eat the debris in the bottom sediments.

Problem: To depict the different food webs in slow- and fast-moving streams.

Materials for the Project:
    six ¼-inch plywood sheets, 6 feet x 18 inches

four ¼-inch plywood sheets, 18 x 18 inches
model railroad grass
box of small finishing nails
rocks
gravel
screening
thick, flexible, clear plastic (must be cuttable and
    moldable)
paints (watercolor is fine)
paintbrushes
scissors
razor blades or artist's knife
cotton
sand
small twigs and branches
pipe cleaners (green)
Elmer's glue
wire
hammer

Methods for the Project:
Make two dioramas, one representing the food web in a fast-moving stream, the other representing the food web in a slow-moving stream.

Construct two boxes for the dioramas. Place one piece of 6-foot x 18-inch plywood on a workbench or on the floor, and put a bead of Elmer's glue along one edge. Glue another piece of plywood, 6 feet x 18 inches, up to the edge of the first panel. Press the edges together and make certain they are plumb. This done, nail the pieces together. The Elmer's glue will cure and make the pieces inseparable.

This forms two sides of your diorama box. Turn the wood over so that the unattached edge faces the ceiling. Run a bead of Elmer's glue along this edge and nail a third piece of 6-foot x 18-inch plywood to this side. Again make certain that the sides are plumb.

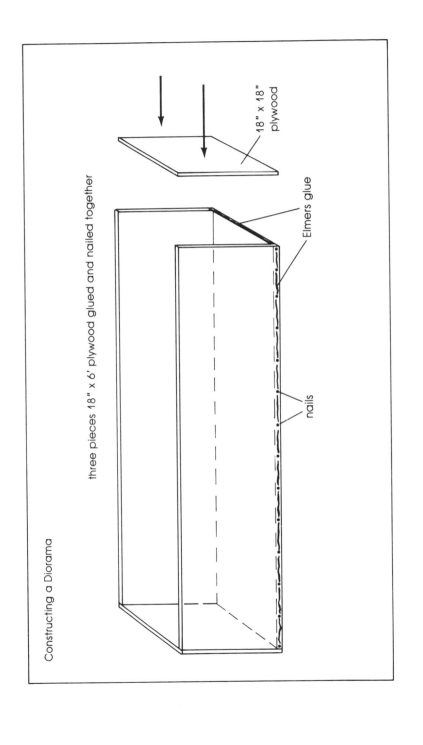

Constructing a Diorama

three pieces 18" x 6' plywood glued and nailed together

18" x 18"
plywood

Elmers glue

nails

Add the sides to the box. Take the 18 x 18-inch pieces of plywood and glue and nail one into the opening on each side of the box.

Make two boxes as described above. One will be for the fast-moving stream and the other for the slow-moving stream. Allow the glue to set overnight.

The first diorama described here will be the fast-moving stream. Using rocks, pebbles, glue, clear plastic, screening, and sand, construct the bed of the stream. It should be very rocky, with many stones sticking out of the water's surface.

The presenter may construct the bottom (bed) of the stream from molded screening covered with papier mâché. The large rocks, pebbles, and sand may be glued to the molded bottom. The brook trout, darters, and sculpins may be painted on the wood background below the water's surface. A wilderness background should be painted on the rear of the box above the water line. The insects (larva and pupa stages) may be painted on the rocks. (Pictures of these animals may be obtained from any wildlife encyclopedia.) Algae and diatoms may be painted on the large rocks. Model railroad grass may be glued to the other side of the rocks to depict the water moss. The surface of the water is molded from clear plastic. These, of course, are only suggestions. The presenter may use any methods, mediums, or ideas that he or she feels will be attractive. All objects in the diorama should be labeled.

Explanation
This diorama represents a fast-moving stream. Organic matter travels with the current to the various organisms depicted on or under the rocks. These organisms are, in turn, eaten by the darters and sculpins, which are eaten by the brook trout. All the organisms in the riffles require cold water, with a high dissolved oxygen content. Water moss grows on the protected side of the large rocks, while

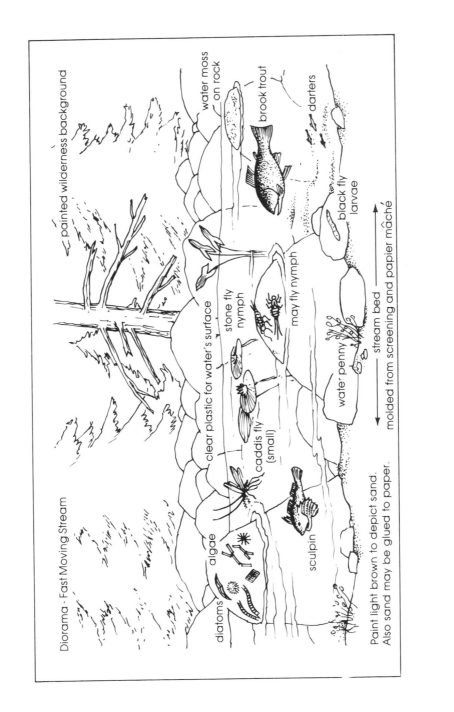

Diorama - Fast Moving Stream

painted wilderness background

water moss on rock

brook trout

darters

black fly larvae

clear plastic for water's surface

stone fly nymph

may fly nymph

water penny

stream bed
molded from screening and papier mâché

caddis fly (small)

algae

diatoms

sculpin

Paint light brown to depict sand.
Also sand may be glued to paper.

hardier algae grows in the direct force of the current. Diatoms also grow on the large rocks. Often the brook trout spend the day in deep holes in the stream, but they come to the riffles to feed. The insects live on or under the rocks of the stream. Minnows, such as the darters and sculpins, have strong front fins to brace themselves against the current.

Explanation
This diorama represents a slow-moving stream. Organic matter settles to the bottom, creating a thick sediment of decomposing material. Plants are anchored to the bottom by their roots. Minnows, bacteria, and small animals eat the plants and decomposing material. These are then eaten by the larger fish. The crayfish and bullheads eat carrion and worms from the bottom. Because the oxygen content is low, bloodworms live at the bottom of the stream. These worms wave back and forth in the water to obtain oxygen and nutrients. The insects are eaten by bluegills and other fish, and even other insects.

Presentation at Fair:
The researcher should present this project by displaying the dioramas side by side with a written explanation of each. Actual photographs of life in fast-moving and slow-moving streams should be displayed in the background of the booth. An audio tape explaining each diorama may be kept running for the viewers' benefit.

THE EFFECTS OF MUNICIPALITIES AND INDUSTRY ON WATER

Because people are terrestrial organisms, we tend to forget the importance of the water ecosystems to the biosphere. The aqueous substance covers three-fourths of the globe.

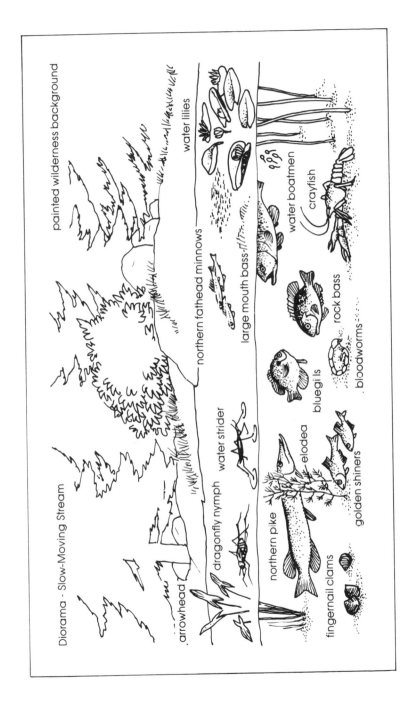

Diorama - Slow-Moving Stream

painted wilderness background

water lilies

northern fathead minnows

large mouth bass

water boatmen

crayfish

rock bass

bloodworms

bluegils

elodea

water strider

dragonfly nymph

arrowhead

northern pike

golden shiners

fingernail clams

Our weather, which reflects the state of the atmosphere, is dependent on and affected by the vast surfaces of the oceans. The unique characteristics of water make it a medium for life and a major component of living substances. It is a universal solvent and absorbs minerals, gases, and nutrients required by living organisms. Water forms valuable mineral rocks and, for years, has served to transport human goods.

Because water absorbs foreign matter easily, it is also easily polluted by nature and people. The hydrologic cycle, the liquid part of the biosphere, transports the wastes and poisons of society throughout the world.

People have progressed to boundaries beyond the atmospheric borders, and yet we still have much to learn here on Earth. It is important for us to understand our aqueous boundaries, to explore them as we have studied medicine, and to discover how to keep them in functional good health.

One need go no farther than the local riverbank to observe the effects of industry on water. Our waterways have been used as dumping grounds and sewers for hundreds of years. People once thought it was impossible to soil this vast ecosystem that stretched for miles before the eyes. It was infinite, a natural resource that would always be there to be defiled.

Industry is responsible for 65 percent of the water pollution in the United States. Manufacturers that use water to produce their goods send the liquid back to its source in a fetid, unsanitary state. The effluent is deadly to people and all other living things. Instead of being two parts hydrogen and one part oxygen, the liquid transmutes into an acidic marsh filled with chemicals, solvents, pesticides, and metals. Its virulent vapor rises into the atmosphere and fouls the air of the city and countryside.

Municipalities are responsible for 20 percent of our water-pollution problem. The major source of municipal pollution stems from untreated or partially treated sewage that is dumped into our waterways, lakes, and oceans. This untreated material, called nonpoint pollution, leads to an overabundance of nutrients in the water, which, in turn, causes an overabundance of vegetation. Vegetable matter dies and decomposes at the bottom. The decomposers use the dissolved oxygen in the water, denying the precious gas to other organic matter. The result: an eutrophic lake, pond, or river, dying or dead before its time. Dissolved oxygen is essential to aquatic life. Most forms of pollution reduce the dissolved oxygen content in water.

Problem: How does municipal nonpoint pollution reduce the dissolved oxygen content of water?

Materials for the Project:
    three 20-gallon fish tanks
    water
    methylene blue indicator solution (tests for dissolved oxygen)
    high-phosphate detergents (Axion, Biz, Tide, or Bold)
    several elodea or other submerged aquatic plants
    gravel
    lights
    timer
    medicine droppers
    two graduated beakers
    test tubes

Methods for the Project:
Put gravel in each fish tank (approximately 4 inches (10 cm) deep). Plant at least four bunches of elodea in each tank, burying the roots deep info the gravel. Fill with

water, and set a lamp over each tank. The tanks should receive approximately fifteen hours of light per day. Set your timer for all three lamps. Label one tank A, one B, and one C, for control. Allow the tanks to stand for a week.

Transfer twenty drops from each tank into the appropriately labeled test tube: A, B, or C. To each test tube add three drops of methylene blue solution. Record the results in a daily log. A deep blue color indicates that it contains a good amount of dissolved oxygen.

Repeat the above process every day for two weeks. Keep a log, recording the appearance of the tanks over this period of time. At the end of the two-week period fill three test tubes one-quarter full of water from each tank. Add three drops of methylene blue solution to each test tube. Record the results. Continue this experiment for at least one month.

Fill two beakers each with 250 milliliters of water. Label one beaker A, the other B. Add 125 milliliters of detergent to beaker A and 125 milliliters of a different detergent to beaker B. This will make a 50 percent mixture of solution. From beaker A add forty drops of the soapy solution to tank A. Do the same to tank B. Do not add any detergent to the control tank.

Presentation at Fair:
Display the three tanks as they appear after one month. The log should also be displayed so that viewers can refer to what is happening in the tanks. In a test-tube rack, display the methylene blue solution test. Photographs of eutrophic bodies of water will enhance your display. The presenter, via a table of values or graphs, may also wish to display statistics on the cost of cleanup as compared to proper sewage facilities for municipalities.

**Other Projects on
Water Pollution:**
You may wish to do further research into industrial, munic-

ipal, or agricultural water pollution. Projects can be developed on oil seepage, thermal pollution, chemical toxification, and pesticides. Each of the aforementioned subjects can lead to interesting and challenging projects.

PESTICIDES AND WATER POLLUTION

Pesticides are insidious and pervasive, as they spread throughout the Earth's water supplies. Persistent chemicals, such as DDT and chlorinated hydrocarbons, are not biodegradable. They remain in the ecosystem for many years. Only recently have we begun to comprehend the effects of these egregious insecticides.

DDT was developed during World War II as a new miracle product to kill the mosquito, which carried the disease malaria. Initially, it proved to be effective in controlling the mosquito and, for the duration of the war, Allied troops experienced relief from the disease.

After World War II the use of DDT spread to domestic agriculture, where it was used by crop growers to combat insect populations. Again the chemical proved to be initially effective. It was then used by municipalities to combat the Dutch elm beetle. The use of DDT and its chemical relatives became widespread.

At the time of the insecticide's development, chemists did not understand that insects rapidly develop immunity to poisons. DDT worked very well on the first several generations, but insect populations change quickly. Some insects reproduce several generations in one season. Due to this fecundity, insects that survived the chemical passed on the immunity. Within a very short time, new insect populations were born that were not affected by DDT and its chemical relatives.

Other species of animals, especially birds, did not escape the effects of DDT. Because the chemical is persistent, it remained in the ground and in the waters and was transferred from one species to another via the food web. Herbivores ingested the chemical, while carnivores and omnivores received doses from animals that ate the contaminated vegetation.

Why is DDT so pernicious? For one thing, the chemical is nonsoluble in water. It is fat soluble only. All living things, plant and animal, contain fat. DDT tends to concentrate in these fatty tissues. Experiments have demonstrated that this concentration has affected the process of photosynthesis among certain forms of algae in the sea.

Because DDT is persistent, it does not break down into harmless substances in the soil or living tissues. DDT is biologically active: It enters the physiological processes of many organisms. In some organisms the chemical is changed to DDE, a virulent substance that, in birds, affects the production of calcium carbonate, the material that makes up eggshells.

As DDT runs off the surface of the Earth, it enters the hydrologic cycle via rivers, percolation to groundwater, and precipitation. Eventually the chemical is well established within the Earth's finite water supply. Because it is not water soluble, the chemical floats in the water. As plankton absorb water to obtain nutrients, they also absorb this toxic chemical, and it becomes part of the fatty tissues in their bodies. These tiny plants are then eaten by the minute animals in the watery ecosystem. They absorb the DDT from the plants they ingest into the fatty tissues of their bodies. Then these small animals are eaten by small fish, and the small fish, by larger fish. Eventually, animals at the top of the food web absorb significant amounts of DDT into their systems. Predators, like the bald eagle, at the upper end of the food web, feel the brunt of this invasive chemical.

The bald eagle, for instance, nests and lays eggs. The mother bird sits on the eggs to incubate them, and the paper-thin shells crack. Or, perhaps, some of the eggs laid have no shells. The developing embryos die. DDT, transmuted to DDE, becomes so concentrated within this predator that it prevents the calcium carbonate from developing in the eggshell. The shells are not strong enough to withstand the incubation.

Not only do these broad-spectrum insecticides affect the upper levels of the food web, but since they are not specifically designed to destroy any one particular organism, they also kill predators, insects, and parasites that would normally feed on the insect pests themselves. Thus, they simplify the food web and create instability. The immune strains of insect pests continue to reproduce and populate the biotic community. Soon the ecosystem is overrun with the pest because the natural predators have been destroyed by the pesticide.

During the 1950s a deciduous woodland in Wisconsin was entirely defoliated in one growing season. In the previous decade, the 1940s, there had been large-scale spraying of DDT in Illinois to combat the Dutch elm beetle. This spraying affected a species of bird that wintered in Illinois. During the summer, these birds lived in those Wisconsin woods, where they ate a caterpillar that fed on the leaves of the deciduous trees. The birds were poisoned. The summer the birds vanished, the caterpillars ran rampant and defoliated the entire woodland. In the words of Rachel Carson, "There was a strange stillness."

DDT and the other chlorinated hydrocarbons are not the only persistent chemicals that in some way enter the hydrologic cycle and cause problems. The PCBs, polychlorinated biphenyls, produced and used in many manufacturing processes, are equally toxic and have been linked to cancer among laboratory animals. PCBs enter the waters as effluent from industries, as well as from the burning of plastics. We have yet to experience the full force of PCBs on our environment.

Mercury and lead, toxic to people, have been found in salmon and birds as well as in the snows of tall mountains. The chemicals seem to have invaded the entire biosphere and have the potential to develop into a major biological problem. In the past, when life was simpler, and people lived in greater harmony with nature, harmful mistakes made by humans would be corrected over time by nature. Today, because of the complexity and large amounts of foreign materials invading the biosphere, natural succession cannot keep up with the rapacious habits of civilization. Human societies are altering natural environments throughout the biosphere with little understanding of the long-term effects of their actions.

**Project Ideas for Pesticide
Pollution of Our Waters:**
Present charts showing the levels of toxicity of the various pesticides in popular use today. Explain how some are more toxic than others and why. Explain which types of pesticides are desirable and why. Create an alternative to pesticide use, and develop a hypothetical situation, putting your solutions into practice.

With charts and diagrams, follow the path of DDT or related pesticides through the food web. Demonstrate the broad-spectrum effects the chemical has on the ecosystem and eventually the biosphere.

Create an imaginary regulatory board to supervise the amount of effluents put into the biosphere. Explain how the board would be legally established and from what authority it would obtain its power. Describe how the panel would monitor the environment and how it would go about enforcing its regulations.

OTHER PROJECTS ON WATER

1. Perform a study of marine ecosystems, and create dioramas representing marine environments. Explain how they differ from reshwater ecosystems.

2. Present a study on the desalination of salt water for use in agriculture and municipalities. Explain the problems involved in the process and the benefits it can bring. Con-

struct a model desalination plant, explaining how it functions.

3. Research the water supplies within the continental United States. Draw a map showing states, such as Wisconsin, with an abundance of water and those, such as Arizona, with very little water. Connect this research with the transience of the U. S. population and the shift of industry to the sunbelt. Project the problems these highly populated, waterless states will encounter. Attempt to offer solutions to the problems.

5

PROJECTS ON SOIL AND TERRESTRIAL ECOSYSTEMS

Soil is the thin layer on the Earth's surface that forms the medium for terrestrial communities, as well as the habitat for a mass of life beneath its surface. Soil is a result of the action of wind, weather, water, sunlight, and living organisms upon the rocks of the Earth. Soil is made from life and must support life. It should never be referred to as dirt, for living things grow in and are an integral part of the soil.

There are many varieties of soils, each with its own unique characteristics and each with varying capabilities for life support. Soil formation begins with the weathering of rocks, which are prepared for organic material. Water seeps into cracks and breaks the solid rocks into minute particles, while the wind and sun work at the rocks' surfaces to sliver away bits and pieces.

Lichens and moss grow in the crevices and further disintegrate the rock material. Other plants root themselves in the softer, more inviting particles that have flaked off the parent rock. These pioneer plants grow in the new soil and change its composition through their own biological activity. Weathering continues to act on the soil.

THE MAKEUP OF SOIL
Soil consists of:
1. organic nutrient material
2. minerals and mineral nutrients
3. air spaces or pores

Organic matter makes up only a small portion of the soil (approximately 5 percent). Bacteria and fungi in the organic portions break down the dead and waste material and provide the necessary nitrogen for living vegetation.

About 50 percent of the soil consists of minerals that provide the necessary nutrients (salts) for growth. Air spaces or pores store water, contain oxygen, allow for drainage, and provide space for the roots to develop.

Soil layers are referred to as horizons. The top layer of soil (horizon A) consists of loose organic debris. It is dark and rich in humus. In this layer there is a high concentration of biological activity. Horizon B consists of lighter-colored mineral salts, such as calcium, iron, and aluminum compounds. Horizon C is rock that has yet to be altered by organic activity and weathering.

Problems: What does a prairie horizon look like? How is it formed? What are its properties?

Materials for the Project:
    a 20-gallon fish tank
    digging material
    watering material
    some prairie plants (i.e., buffalo grass)
    dark oilcloth
    glue or silicone sealant
    calcium carbonate
    iron filings
    clay soil
    garden soil
    rich humus-filled soil
    soil pH test kit
    two large boxes (to be set up like a moisture-gradient box, pp. 56–57)
    grass seed

watering pitcher
organic material (grass cuttings, animal wastes,
    dead leaves)

Methods for the Project:
Cut oilcloth to fit over the sides of your fish tank, then glue the oilcloth over the sides. Glue the oilcloth at the top, but allow the bottom to be raised so the soil structure can be seen.

Place a 2-inch (5-cm) layer of rocks and gravel on the bottom of the tank to represent the consolidated bedrock, or unweathered soil. Mix clay soil with calcium carbonate (about 50 percent of each). Layer about 4 inches (10 cm) of this material over the bedrock. Combine garden soil with bits of iron filings and small bits (not many) of organic material, including grass cuttings, dead leaves, and animal wastes. Spread this over the calcium salts. It should be about 4 inches (10 cm) deep. Now add rich humus soil (filled with organic material) over the last layer. Your grassland has been established.

There are many ways in which grassland and other soils are affected by natural occurrences. Weathering and organic action constantly change soil.

One of the major natural effects on soil is erosion, the wearing away of the nutrient-rich top layer by rain, running water, and wind. Erosion, or the combined forces of degradation, also includes gravity and temperature. These two forces crack rocks apart and carry the debris to lower elevations.

Without vegetation soil is extremely vulnerable to rapid erosion. When green is gone and the roots that hold the earth in place are destroyed, what took nature thousands of years to build can vanish within a decade.

Cultivation of soil is a major cause of accelerated erosion. Stripped of its protective vegetable mantle, soil disappears faster than natural forces can replace it. Tillage

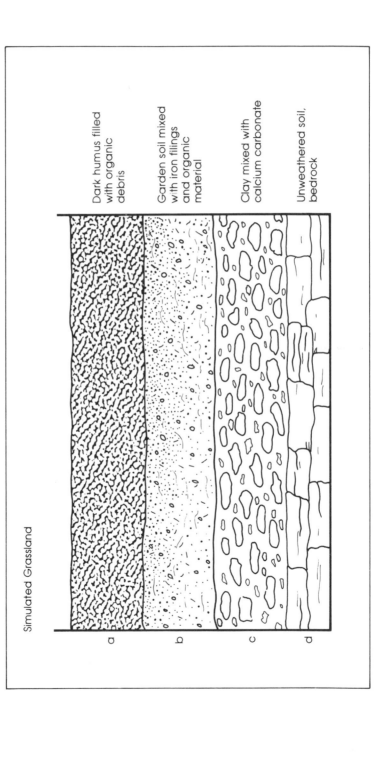

Simulated Grassland

a — Dark humus filled with organic debris

b — Garden soil mixed with iron filings and organic material

c — Clay mixed with calcium carbonate

d — Unweathered soil, bedrock

also exposes the lower, humus-rich materials to the erosive forces, and these nutritive materials are also lost. The land is impoverished and, thus, abandoned by living organisms. Another natural form of soil deterioration is depletion, the removal of nutrient material by rain (leaching) or plant growth.

Nature also affects the pH (acidity-alkalinity) of the soil. Some soils are slightly acid because of rainfall, which is a mild carbonic acid. Rainwater leaches alkaline material. Soils can also be acidic because of the vegetation they support. For example, bog soils tend to be acidic.

Other soils are alkaline because of the way they were formed. Most deserts possess an alkaline soil. As a general rule, damp ecosystems usually have acid soils, while dry communities are alkaline.

Set up two moisture-gradient boxes. Label one box A, the other B. Plant grass seed in box A, and allow time for it to establish itself. Do nothing with box B. Place the two moisture-gradient boxes at one side of your prairie horizon. Display charts on cultivated erosion in front of the boxes. Use a watering pitcher to simulate rain, and water each moisture-gradient box. Box A will demonstrate how vegetation prevents erosion. Box B will serve as your example of erosion caused by tillage.

Test your grassland horizon for acidity. Display samples of the test in front of the horizon, with an explanation of soil pH. You may also have pH samples from other types of soils and dramatize the contrasts.

On the other side of the prairie horizon, display photographs showing how people destroy soil. The photographs should include examples of erosion, pesticide effects, urban sprawl, highway construction, strip mining, and other misuses of natural resources.

Presentation at Fair:
This project is a generalized statement on the importance of soil to the biosphere. It should be displayed as was sug-

gested before, with well-researched photographs and captions. The complexity of this project is up to you. You can go as far as presenting films on the dust bowls of the 1930s or do as little as showing the horizons and pH tests.

PROJECT ON RESOURCE USE—
RECYCLING PAPER

As stated earlier, erosion has been extended by people's mismanagement of the land. Over the ages people have assumed that they are the single most important organism within the biosphere and that all other organisms were developed for their benefit and use. Only recently have we discovered that the resources of the planet are finite and that it is our responsibility to guard against misuse and ensure preservation. This, of course, can be accomplished only through thoughtful conservation practices.

With this in mind, modern civilizations are beginning to legislate against the destruction of the natural environment. Environmental impact studies are now required for most major construction projects. Pesticides can no longer be sprayed recklessly, and sewage systems must pass strict standards.

We have also discovered that our traditional forms of energy, long believed to be available in unlimited quantities, are limited. Projects under way seek new, pollution-free forms of energy, energy that will ensure our future. Solar energy systems are being developed at several major universities, as well as by private industry. And there is research in progress on fusion, the energy source of the sun.

Societies today have also become aware of the need to save. Nature does not produce garbage, but people do. Now humans, like nature, are learning to recycle their wastes. Aluminum cans can be used innumerable times, garbage can be burned as fuel, and paper can be recycled.

Paper is one of the most useful materials in the modern-day world. Its value to society is immeasurable, as it is used to spread knowledge and information and to keep records. Paper is also used in the construction of homes and buildings, in packaging, in medicine, and in a multitude of other ways far too numerous to mention here.

Most paper today is manufactured from cellulose fiber, a substance found in most plants. Forests are logged, and tree trunks are sent to the mill, where they are cut to a workable size, and their bark is removed. The wood is then thoroughly washed and cut into small chips. The chips move over screens that sift out remaining pieces of bark and other impurities. They are then ready for the semichemical process of pulp-making (the soda process).

The chips are deposited in a machine called a digester (approximately 24 to 30 feet (7.2 to 9 m) tall). Here the chips are cooked at extremely high temperatures with a mixture of water and sodium hydroxide. The caustic soda dissolves the materials that hold the cellulose. Different woods are cooked for varying periods of time, depending upon the type of paper being manufactured. Pulp is derived from this process.

The wood pulp is washed to remove chemical residue (resin, lignin, sap, and lye). Next, the pulp is bleached in a solution of chlorine and hypochlorite. These treatments occur in several successive tanks. The pulp becomes a tannish color, as more of the lye and other chemicals are washed out. This process continues until the pulp becomes almost pure white.

The pulp is now ready for beating. The beater is a circular vat, which rubs and presses on the cellulose pulp as it passes through. Next the pulp enters the Jordan machine. During this procedure the fibers are brushed and cut to various lengths. Now to the Fourdrinier, which forms the fluffy, wet pulp into a matted sheet. This sheet is dried over suction boxes and then steam-heated as it passes over rollers.

The cylinder machine rolls and presses the fibers. It is during this process that the paper is watermarked. Except for certain printing papers, all fine paper receives this mark. The paper is now rolled onto cylinders and is ready to be weighed into standard reams.

The procedure for recycling paper is similar to the original papermaking process. The used paper is broken down into pulp and then treated in the same manner as original wood pulp. Recycled paper is used for writing paper, tissue, newsprint, and many other products.

Recycling of paper became necessary when, in the mid-1970s, it became apparent that the paper industry could not keep up with consumer demand. Also, there has been a greater awareness by Americans of the need for conservation. We now recognize the need to preserve our forests as well as our other natural resources. This can be accomplished only by finding new and better techniques for using and reusing materials that are readily available.

Problem: How can paper be recycled?

Materials for the Project:
electric blender
rolling pin
framed piece of aluminum or cloth screening
  (6 × 6 feet)
bowl or vat (24 × 36 inches)
blotting paper (to be used to dry recycled
  paper)
iron
cheesecloth
newspaper or tissue (newspaper makes a better
  quality paper)
distilled water
sponge

Methods for the Project:

Prepare newspaper for recycling by cutting a large amount of paper in small slivers. Put distilled water into the blender, enough to cover the blades, and then add the slivers of newspaper. Blend the paper and water for approximately one to two minutes. Add more water and blend again for thirty seconds.

Pour the contents into the bowl. Submerge one of the screened frames into the bowl. Hold it under the water and agitate the frame back and forth. The pulp will cling to the screening. Remove the frame and hold it over the bowl to allow water to drip. Place a sheet of blotting paper over the wet pulp on the screen. Press it down gently so that it absorbs some of the excess water and forces some back into the bowl.

Moisten a sponge, and press down on the blotter. This will remove more water. Lift the paper off the screen by grasping the edge and carefully pulling it back.

Put the new sheet of paper down on a dry blotter and cover it with another dry blotter. Using the sponge remove more water from the sheet. Squeeze out more water with a rolling pin. Roll lightly several times over the sheets.

Put the new sheet of paper between two wet blotters and cover these with cheesecloth. Iron the sheet, turning constantly, for approximately three to five minutes. Remove the new sheet of paper from the blotters.

Presentation at Fair:

Previously recycled paper should be displayed with documentation as to how it was made. The actual recycling process should take place at a center table. Recycle your paper once an hour. This project should be part of a display on conservation of resources. Show photographs of recent conservation policies, for example, home insulation, better waste management, and use of alternate fuel sources, along with the rationale for conservation.

AN ENVIRONMENTAL SYSTEM

People's intrinsic curiosity and their ability to reason have given them an intense interest in the environment and the desire to discover their role in the natural order.

All life on Earth exists within the biosphere, and the biosphere conforms to the rules of natural law. The human being, like all other living organisms, must find its specific niche within this system. People are omnivores, classified as consumers at the third trophic level within the food web. They are vertebrates, mammals, primates, and, finally, homo sapiens. But these classifications do not define their role within the natural order. The ability to reason, to think creatively, and to solve problems separates people from other organisms within the biosphere.

The behavior of all animals can be defined roughly with two terms or concepts: *egocentric behavior,* that is, behavior directed inward toward the self; and *social behavior,* behavior directed outward toward others of the same and other species. A person has these two characteristics along with a a third: *emotional behavior,* based on feelings.

Egocentric behavior includes feeding, maintenance, shelter, and self-defense. Social behavior is manifested in sexual, community, parental, and competitive relationships. Both egocentric and social behavior are important in determining how an animal adapts to changes within its environment.

Selection of Environmental System:

An environmental model may be constructed to represent any typical biome or ecosystem. Ideally it should typify a biome and contain, within the biome, several examples of specific ecosystems. This environmental system will demonstrate the broad concept of ecological interrelationships through specific concepts of change, diversity, adaptation, symbiosis, carrying capacity, and others.

One typical example of a biome is a deciduous forest, or a woodland, which contains four major ecosystems: a pond or lake, a river, a freshwater marsh, and various forms of plant life. There are also minor ecosystems: a rotting log, life under a rock, a rock pile within the pond, the subterranean ecosystem, and life within a decomposing pile of leaves. The pond, marsh, and river are designed to represent a typical environment within any given deciduous forest (north central to northeastern United States).

You may present any biome within the biosphere. The construction will be the same except for specific areas. Remember to research the biome thoroughly and to pay attention to the hours of sunlight, soil structure, and moisture and temperature requirements.

Problem: How does a balanced community function?

Materials for the Project:
    a 50-gallon fish tank
    two sheets of glass, both the width of the tank
        (one a third the height of the tank, and the
        other, half the height of the tank)
    silicone sealant
    wood for framing
    screening
    a small submergible recirculating water pump
    hose or tubing for pump
    heat lamp
    an electric timer
    fiberglass cloth
    fiberglass resin and hardener
    disposable paintbrushes
    gravel
    marsh soil
    woodland soil (high in nutrients)
    stapler
    rocks

submergible plants (elodea, myrophyllum)
marsh plants (iris, marsh marigold, venus flytrap,
    pitcher plant, marsh grass, sneezeweed,
    arrowhead)
woodland plants (wood violet, wood vine,
    deadly nightshade, lady fern, cinnamon fern,
    black-eyed Susan, trillium, skunk cabbage,
    bloodroot, May apple, columbine). If your
    tank is large enough, you might put in some
    small shrubs (dogwood, witch hazel)
pond animals (bluegill, bullhead, crayfish)
marsh animals (painted turtle, leopard frog)
woodland animals (garter snake, salamander,
    cricket)

Methods for the Project:
Clean the tank to remove dust and foreign particles.
Place the glass sheet (the one that is a third the height of
the tank) into the tank to cut off one-fourth of the space.
Glue this glass in place with the silicone. This second area,
also one-fourth of the tank, will be the freshwater marsh.
The remainder of the tank will be woodland.

Divide the tank in half with the second sheet of glass.
Glue this glass in place with the silicone. This second area, also one-fourth of the tank, will be the freshwater marsh. The remainder of the tank will be woodland.

Allow twenty-four hours for the silicone to set. Now
cover the bottom of the marsh and woodland areas with
coarse gravel. The gravel beds should be at least 2 inches
(5 cm) thick. Fill the woodland with the proper soil.

Soil in the woodland should go from the glass divider
to two-thirds the height of the tank.

Soil in the marsh area should run at a 45-degree angle
from the woodland to 2 inches (5 cm) below the edge of
the glass dividing the woodland from the pond.

Place a 2-inch (5-cm) layer of gravel in the bottom of
the pond. Also put gravel in the marsh area up to the

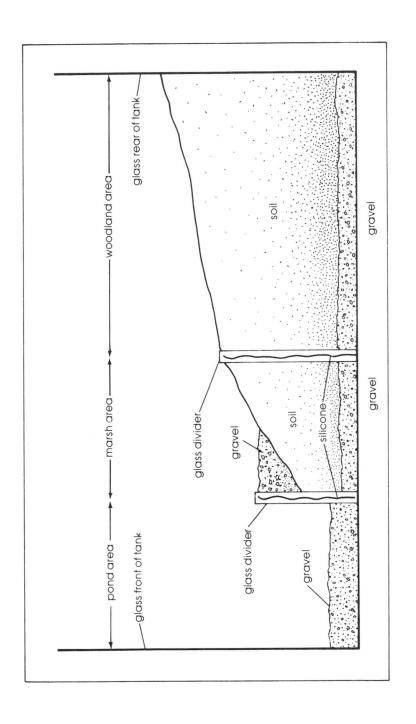

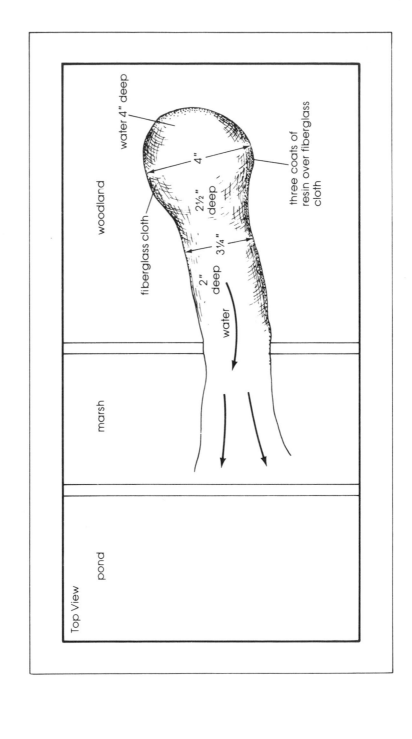

Top View

pond

marsh

woodland

water

2" deep

3¼"

fiberglass cloth

2½" deep

4"

water 4" deep

three coats of resin over fiberglass cloth

edge of the glass divider to prevent soil from washing into the pond.

In an area of your choice, in the woodland section, scoop out a 4-inch-deep (10-cm), 4-inch-diameter hole. Then remove a 3-inch-wide (7.5-cm), 2-inch-deep (5-cm) section from the marsh area. This will become your riverbed.

Lay screen into the mold. (Do not worry about buckles in the screening. This will simulate natural formations.) Cover the screening with fiberglass cloth. Staple the cloth at the upper edges to the screening after laying the cloth. Give it a minimum of three coats of fiberglass resin (follow directions on can).

Submerge your small recirculating pump in the pond and run the tubing underground from the pond to the small hollow in the upland. If you choose, you may put rocks about the pond in the upland and run the tubing into the rocks, thus creating a waterfall.

Fill the pond and test to see if the river system is functional. Adjust to personal taste. The pond should flow over the glass divider to create a shallow-water area in the marsh.

Plant your vegetation. Allow approximately ten to fourteen days for the vegetation to stabilize and establish root systems. The pond vegetation will require less time to establish itself than the marsh or woodland vegetation.

Soil in a woodland rarely dries out. Marsh soil is always soggy. Research the environmental conditions necessary for the plants that you use.

While the plants are establishing themselves, construct a screened top for the system. Design the frame so that it completely covers the tank. The frame should be constructed like a door or window frame. The top frame will rest on the lower frame, which should be fitted around the top of the tank. It should be at least 2 feet (.6 m) high and have a small door over the pond area. This height will allow space for the woodland plants to grow. The door will be for feeding the pond animals.

Side View

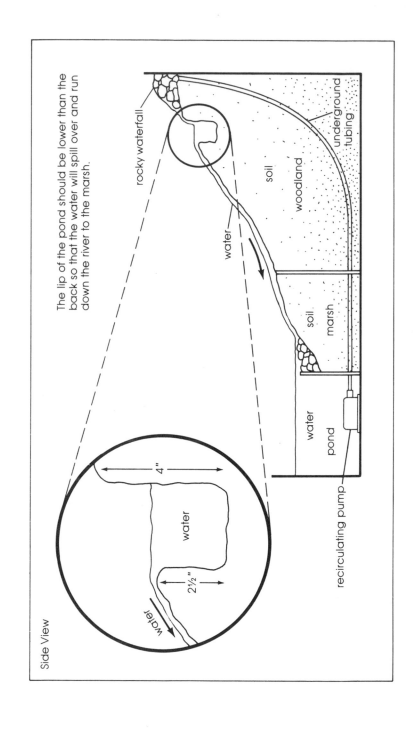

The lip of the pond should be lower than the back so that the water will spill over and run down the river to the marsh.

rocky waterfall

water

soil

woodland

underground tubing

soil

marsh

water

pond

recirculating pump

water

4"

2½"

water

The insects should be the first animal life introduced into the environmental system. This will allow them to establish themselves and lay eggs to ensure future generations. Wait a week and then add the fish and other animals, such as turtles, garter snakes, worms, salamanders, leopard frogs, crayfish, tadpoles, and toads. The environmental system is now ready for observation and experiment.

OBSERVATIONS AND EXPERIMENTS FOR THE ENVIRONMENTAL SYSTEM

As was said previously, food webs are an integral part of all biomes and ecosystems and are intrinsic within the definition of ecology. Ecology is the study of how all living things interrelate via the food web. All biomes have food webs based upon grazing and transfer solar energy to the system through the producers (green plants). Through the process of photosynthesis, green plants convert light energy to glucose (a simple sugar) and store the glucose within their tissues. This stored energy is transferred to other creatures within the biome via the varying levels of consumers.

First-level consumers are herbivores, animals that eat only green plants. Herbivores are eaten by second-level consumers, carnivores, animals that eat only meat. There are third-level consumers that eat only carnivores, and fourth-level consumers that eat both herbivores and carnivores. At the fifth level lie the omnivores, animals that eat at all the above levels.

Everything that lives must die, and all living things produce waste products. The detrital food web consumes the dead and waste materials of a biome or ecosystem. Bacteria, fungi, certain worms, and flies ingest organic waste and convert it in their bodies into nutrient material. The nutrient material is then passed back into the flow of the biome or ecosystem by being absorbed through the roots of plants and used in the process of photosynthesis.

Keep a daily log on the food web in the pond, marsh, and woodland. The log should reflect the interrelationship between all the living organisms of the microhabitat. The producers in each ecosystem should be listed, as well as the various levels of consumers. A diagram of the food web within a specific area should accompany the log.

The detrital food web should also be logged and diagrammed. Each ecosystem has its own decomposers. If you choose, you may also demonstrate the carbon cycle via the food web.

Carbon is the basic ingredient of all organic compounds. It moves throughout the ecosystem with the flow of energy through the food web. The basic source of all carbon is carbon dioxide gas, which is found in the atmosphere and dissolved in water.

The first step in the carbon cycle is the process of photosynthesis. Plants absorb carbon dioxide through their stomata, openings in the undersides of the leaf, and water through their roots. In the presence of light, plants convert the water and carbon dioxide into simple sugars (carbohydrates). These are then converted into complex fats, complex sugars (polysaccharides), proteins, and vitamins.

Plants are ingested by herbivores, which synthesize these complex fats and sugars into other carbon compounds. The carnivores eat the herbivores and resynthesize these compounds once again.

Carbon is returned to the atmosphere as a by-product of the respiratory processes of animals. The carbon within the tissues of the plants and animals is eventually released by the breakdown of dead and waste materials. Most of this carbon eventually returns to the atmosphere and water as carbon dioxide gas. Some carbon remains in the soil as coal, oil, or natural gas. This carbon is consequently removed from the cycle for a long time, until it is released by humans in energy consumption.

Carrying capacity also affects the food chain within any specific ecosystem. The carrying capacity is the maximum number of any given species that can be supported within an ecosystem. Once organisms reach the carrying capacity of the habitat, they begin to exhaust the food supply and eventually suffer a severe population decrease due to starvation and disease.

Pick any ecosystem within an environmental system and introduce an overabundance of any species of plant or animal. The system should then be observed and the data logged. This may be presented at the fair via photographs of the results.

Adaptation. All plants and animals are specifically adapted to their given environments. Keep a chart on the specific adaptations of the animals in the pond, marsh, and woodland. Diagrams showing unique adaptations of individual species, such as a snake's unhinged jaw, which allows it to swallow prey larger than itself, may be displayed.

Diversity is necessary to the health and well-being of any biome or ecosystem. In order to be successful, a community must be diverse. Homogeneous communities (without people's intervention) are seldom successful. Even within climax ecosystems, one finds an aggregation of species. A deciduous forest often contains beech, oak, hickory, and others. No one species appears dominant. But, even within virgin stands, the dominant species make up only 25 to 30 percent of the life forms.

Symbiosis is a classic form of adaptation in which two or more species of plants or animals form a close relationship to one another. The relationship is usually so close as to be necessary to the survival of the organisms.

You may have diagrams of the various examples of symbiosis within the environmental system. These relationships can be observed and logged, the charts demonstrating the duration of the relationships.

One kind of symbiosis is *mutualism*, a relationship in which both species involved benefit. Each species helps the other in a certain way—for example, the bee and the flower. The bee gathers pollen to manufacture honey. In turn, as the bee flies from flower to flower, it spreads pollen and thus fertilizes the plants.

Another example is the rhinoceros and the tickbird. The tickbird sits on the rhino's back and eats the ticks. The rhinoceros provides a food supply for the bird, and the bird in turn rids the huge beast of irritating pests.

Finally, a classic example of a mutualistic relationship is the lichen—a combination of an alga and a fungus working together to form a unique partnership. The alga provides chlorophyll for photosynthesis, while the fungus provides moisture. Together these organisms cling to a tree or rock.

Commensalism is a symbiotic relationship in which one organism benefits while the other is neither helped nor harmed. An example of this type of relationship is the pilot fish and the shark. The pilot fish is seen constantly swimming with the shark. When the shark makes a kill, the pilot fish is there to pick up the bits and pieces. The pilot fish benefits, and the shark is neither helped nor harmed.

Parasitism is the least understood of the three symbiotic relationships. With parasitism, one organism, the parasite, benefits; the other organism (the host) is harmed. Often parasitism is confused with predation. The difference between the two is that a predator kills its prey and instantly eats it, while a parasite feeds off the living host. Once the host organism dies, it is of no use to the parasite. Thus, a small parasite kills its host very slowly. An example of parasitism is the strangler fig tree and a fig tree. The strangler wraps itself around the giant fig tree and sucks nourishment from its body. Eventually the strangler becomes too large and kills the host. Within the animal kingdom one can find numerous examples of parasitism: the lamprey eel and the salmon, for example, or the wood tick and the deer.

Homogeneous systems tend to be the result of competition between two or more species or the intervention of human beings. For example, until the 1950s most urban environments in the northeastern and midwestern United States were planted with American elm trees. When the Dutch elm beetle, introduced to this country in the 1930s, invaded, it easily spread from tree to tree. Because the American elm trees were planted close together and in homogeneous stands, the beetle had a field day. Now the American elm is endangered.

Had the city planners taken a lesson from nature, they would have planted the streets with a diversity of species. The natural barriers would have slowed the parasite's progress and allowed time for resistance to develop.

Create a chart demonstrating the diversity of species within the communities of an environmental system. The data logged, you can show how species diversity has strengthened the system.

OTHER PROJECTS ON ECOSYSTEMS

Photosynthesis. Do a project based on the photosynthetic equation, demonstrating how each step in this process works. Perform experiments to prove each part of the equation, and then link this to its specific application within the food chain.

Habitats. Design minihabitats representing ecosystems from one biome or several different biomes. Demonstrate the food chain, adaptation, carrying capacity, etc.

Birds of Prey. With photographs of empty nests or broken eggshells, demonstrate how various birds of prey have been affected by the use of pesticides. Use charts and tables to show how these birds reached near extinction levels and are now attempting a comeback. Present the various methods practiced today to help these birds survive.

BIOLOGICAL CLOCKS IN PLANTS AND ANIMALS

All living things respond to stimuli from the sun. In plants and animals this response is referred to as *photoperiodism*. People have artificially created years, based upon the Earth's rotation about the sun. The years are divided into seasons, based upon the hours of sunlight falling on the Earth each day. The shortest day of the year, December 22, marks the winter solstice and the beginning of winter. The winter months continue, with the days getting longer, until day and night are equal in length. The spring equinox, March 21, marks an equal day and night and begins the spring season. During the spring months the days continue to lengthen, until the longest day of the year marks the summer solstice, June 21. Then the days grow shorter until the length of day equals that of night, the autumn equinox. The days continue to shorten until, once again, the winter solstice is upon us.

These seasons occur in the temperate zones of the Earth. Elsewhere on the planet there are different seasons. The tundra, for example, has only two seasons: winter and summer, dark and light. The tropics have but one season, marked by wet and dry periods. The Southern Hemisphere's seasons are the opposite of those in the Northern.

Most plants on the planet respond to the amount of light they receive from the sun. Deciduous forests lie dormant during the winter months and do not sprout leaves until the amount of daylight increases in the spring. The entire community within a deciduous forest depends upon the amount of light that filters through the canopy of branches and leaves overhead. The variety of light is what provides for the development of one or more states of undergrowth.

In the early spring, late March or early April, the first plants emerge. Early spring bloomers, such as wild onions and skunk cabbage, grow before the canopy begins to form overhead. They live their entire life cycle before the large trees bloom. These first hardy plants are followed by the forest wildflowers in late April and early May. These flowers, such as trillium, violet, and Solomon's seal, bloom in the spring just as buds are burgeoning from the hardwood trees overhead.

As the canopy begins to form, the shrub layer of the forest comes to life. Shrubs live beneath the canopy and are adapted to survive on less light than the trees overhead. By late May or early June the canopy is well developed. The wildflowers of spring have bloomed and have gone through their cycles.

All plants can be put into one of three photoperiodic categories: *short-day plants, long-day plants*, and *day-neutral plants*. Both short-day and long-day plants are influenced by the amount of sunlight they receive daily. Day-neutral plants are not controlled by light but by age. The plants flower when the amount of sunlight has reached the right stage. This is called the *critical day length*. The critical day length varies for different plants in a forest, but as you can see, for spring flowers it is much shorter than for the climax hardwood trees.

Spring flowers in the forest are considered short-day plants because they bloom before the summer solstice. Long-day plants, like many in the prairies and meadows, bloom late in the season, after the summer solstice. Day-neutral plants may bloom at any time, depending upon the species.

All these plants, and animals, too, respond to light. Light is the stimulating or prohibiting agent of their development. For example, if a short-day plant were to be removed from its environment and stimulated with light, it would stop blooming, while a long-day plant, under these artificial conditions, would continue to bloom.

Rhythms exist for animals as well as for plants. Herbivores respond to the seasonal periodicities of plants. Carnivores, in turn, respond to these periodicities through the herbivores. In lean years the timber wolf has been known not to breed. Studies demonstrate that there is a direct correlation between the size of the timber wolf's litter and the amount of food available during the year.

Many people assume that temperature triggers the biological clocks within plants and animals. This has been proven to be untrue. Most biological changes are stimulated by light. The snowshoe hare, for example, will turn white when the amount of daylight decreases. It does not matter what the temperature is or whether there is any snow on the ground.

All species, including people, are sensitive to an internal biological clock. Stimulated by the length of the day or the night, this clock regulates almost all the major functions within a given species of plant or animal.

PHOTOPERIODIC PROJECTS AT FAIRS
Present an experiment in which short-day and long-day plants are put in a controlled environment. Demonstrate how long-day plants continue to bloom when stimulated by light, while short-day plants will stop blooming. Prepare charts on short-day and long-day bloomers to illustrate your findings.

Outline the rutting cycle of the white-tailed deer to demonstrate how its mating and reproductive habits are directly related to the length of day. The breeding cycle of this animal is definitely connected to the decreasing length of the day in autumn.

6

HUMAN POPULATION AND THE ENVIRONMENT

Before people became a recognizable force on the planet Earth, there was a harmonious balance between the physical and biological parts of the biosphere. The transfer of energy occurred spontaneously through food webs, while nutrients were recycled through the natural systems without interference. Communities were diverse, containing thousands of species of plants and animals, which insured their stability.

At first people did little to alter the biosphere's diversified balance. They were mainly hunters and food gatherers, their numbers were small, and they killed only enough to feed and clothe their small communities. Early humans, an integral part of an ecosystem, complemented the environment. Nutrients depleted by these communities of people were returned to the system in a natural manner.

Early human beings had a life expectancy of approximately thirty to thirty-five years. This short life span, coupled with a high infant mortality rate, regulated the human population as it did other organisms within the environment. Human populations remained stable until the middle of the nineteenth century.

The beginning of the Industrial Revolution brought with it a better standard of living for many of the world's peoples. Modern medicine conquered diseases that af-

fected children. As a result more children lived to become adults and bear children of their own.

Medicine and science combined to create better living conditions. Medicine cured diseases that had been fatal in the past. Science made milk safe to drink, developed refrigeration, and brought about higher crop yields.

These factors led to two phenomena: The human population began to increase drastically (plus, since the 1900s, the average life expectancy has increased by twenty-five years), and technology has removed the human being more and more from the natural environment. These events, among others, have led us toward a world in crisis today.

Today, 14 percent of the mammals in the United States are endangered. Each year the percentage rises with the loss of habitat. DDT affected many birds. Today, still on shaky ground, the birds are attempting a comeback. If the human population continues to grow at its present rate, someday there will be no room on Earth for wildlife. The Earth will consist of people, cows, cement, and corn. It will become a well-managed factory, geared to the production of people and their support systems.

For the first four thousand years of human existence, the population increased to approximately 5 million (8000 B.C. to 4000 B.C. At this time in their history, humans developed agriculture, which made it possible to feed more people. By the time of Christ, the Earth's population was up to 135 million. It took another 1,500 years for the Earth's population to reach 500 million.

From 1650 to 1850 the world's population doubled and reached 1 billion. This, of course, was because of the Renaissance and Industrial Revolution. The population next doubled in only eighty years, by 1930. The Earth today has 4.2 billion people, and experts project that by the year 2000 there will be over 7 billion people, and by 2015, over 10 billion.

This exponential growth pattern adds 200,000 more people to the biosphere every day—200,000 more mouths to feed and people to house, 200,000 users of energy, 200,000 polluters. Some biologists think that the Earth, by the year 2015, will be very different from what it is at present. There will be no national wildlife areas, no parks, no geese flying overhead. Instead, there will be cities—perhaps one large city. A monstrous urban sprawl. The air will have a constant yellow haze as it hangs over this homogeneous environment. There will be managed fields of crops and terraced or leveled farming techniques. The animals will be cows, pigs, and perhaps sheep. There will be no birds. Birds would compete with people for food. They will have to go, as will the predators and the wild herbivores.

The normal food web will be bypassed, and everything within the biosphere will exist only for human survival.

Food. If one were to take all the food produced in the world today and divide it equally among all the peoples of the Earth, everyone would be hungry. There is not enough food produced now to feed the present world population. Imagine the Earth as a pie, and imagine all the people invited to the party of life getting a piece. If you have too many people at the party, the piece will be too small. You must buy another pie. Where can we get another pie? What happens when all the pie is gone? Will you be able to live on your piece of pie?

Energy. We have already observed the problems of massive energy consumption. But energy is the least of our problems. Alternative energy sources can and will be developed, but where will our technology find more land? Will our scientists be able to develop alternative food sources?

Housing. With today's urban sprawl and the construction of highways, we are in the paradoxical position of needing more land to produce food for the growing human population and, at the same time, needing more land for the development of metropolitan areas. The problem is becoming critical. Each new home reduces wild habitat and farmland, both needed for human survival. The exponential growth of the human population, like a parasite destroying its host, is eating up the land.

People have evolved as an integral part of nature. Within each human being the need to belong still exists. Even the most sophisticated among us still possess the desire to be one with nature. It is up to us to change the course of life on Earth. How? Maybe you will tell us.

Population Projects at Fairs:

Do a statistical research study on the exponential growth of the human population. Demonstrate graphically how the human population developed. Point out how the Industrial Revolution was a major turning point in human development. Show, through drawings or charts, what the condition of the biosphere will be in the year 2015.

Present a project based upon zero population growth by the year 2000. Via charts and diagrams, demonstrate the correlation between a decreasing human population and the standard of living.

Correlate human population growth with the reduction of wildlife habitat. Demonstrate, through present facts and projections, how the wild is rapidly disappearing.

GLOSSARY

ADAPTATION. The process or processes by which an organism becomes better suited to its environment, or for its particular functions.

AEROSOLS. Particles so small that they remain suspended in the atmosphere for many years.

ATMOSPHERE. The primary layer of gases enshrouding the Earth. A mixture of gases (78 percent nitrogen, 21 percent oxygen, .02 percent carbon dioxide, .08 percent argon, and other rare gases). The air.

AUTOTROPHIS. Organisms capable of producing organic substances from inorganic materials by means of energy received from outside the organisms; e.g., plants with chlorophyll and certain bacteria.

BIOLOGICAL. Pertaining to the organic (living) part of the biosphere.

BIOMASS. The total quantity, at a given time, of living organisms of one or more species, or of all the species in a community.

BIOME. The community of living organisms of a single major ecological region.

BIOSPHERE. The portion of the Earth and its atmosphere that is capable of supporting life.

BIOTIC COMMUNITY. A naturally occurring assemblage of plants and animals that live in the same area and are mutually sustaining and interdependent via the food web.

BOREAL FOREST (TAIGA). The forest consisting chiefly of conifers, extending across North America and Asia.

CARBON CYCLE. The transformation of carbon from carbon dioxide in the atmosphere into sugar by photosynthesis in plants, synthesis of more complex organic compounds in plants and animals, and the return by respiration or death and decay of plant and animal tissues to carbon dioxide.

CARNIVORE. Any animal that eats only flesh.

CARRYING CAPACITY. The maximum number of wildlife species that a specific community will support.

CELLULOSE. The principal component of the cell wall of plants, a complex carbohydrate. Used in the manufacture of paper.

CHAPARRAL. A biome with low and often dense scrub vegetation, characterized by shrubs or dwarf trees such as buckbrush, with mostly evergreen and hard leaves.

CHLOROPHYLL. The green pigment in plants. The only substance capable of converting light energy into chemical energy.

CHLORINATED HYDROCARBONS. A group of persistent chemicals used in the manufacture of certain pesticides.

CIRCADIAN RHYTHMS. Daily cycles of plants and animals.

CLIMAX. The kind of community capable of perpetuation under the prevailing climatic conditions. The terminal stage of a pioneer community.

COMMENSALISM. A symbiotic relationship in which two or more organisms live together with benefit to one and injury to none.

COMMUNITY. A group of one or more populations of plants and animals in a common spatial arrangement.

CONVECTION. Heat transfer in air and liquids. Cool air falls and causes warm air to rise.

CONVECTION CURRENTS. Currents created by the movements of cold and warm air.

DAY-NEUTRAL PLANT. A plant that blooms when the length of day is either long or short. Affected more by age than by light.

DDT. An insecticide, dichloro-diphenyl-trichloro-ethane, which is a colorless, odorless, water-insoluble crystalline.

DECIDUOUS. Refers to losing parts of an organism, such as leaves of trees, e.g., the deciduous forest biome.

DESERT. A biome that has an arid, hot to cool climate, with vegetation that is sparse and usually shrubby.

DETRITAL FOOD WEB. The food web of decay and decomposition. Certain types of bacteria, fungi, insects, and worms recycle nutrients to the plant life of a community.

ECOLOGY. The study of how all organisms interrelate to each other and to their nonliving environment.

ECOSYSTEM. A specialized community, including all the component organisms, that forms an interacting system, e.g., a marsh.

ENERGY. The ability to do work.

ENVIRONMENT. The sum total of all external conditions that may influence organisms.

EUTROPHIC. Bodies of water that may be deficient in oxygen due to an excess of nutrients.

EXPONENTIAL GROWTH. The constant doubling of the human population on Earth.

FOOD WEB. The diagrammatic relationships of organisms within a community and their dependence upon one another for energy in the form of food. Producers (the autotrophic organisms) produce food in the form of sugars, while the herbivores, carnivores, omnivores, and decomposers (the heterotrophic organisms) transfer and transform this energy until it is finally returned to the carbon or nitrogen cycles.

GRASSLAND. A biome consisting chiefly of grasses or grasslike plants. Prairies, steppes, savannas, velds and pampas are grasslands.

GRASSLIKE PLANT. A plant that resembles a true grass, e.g., sedges or rushes.

GROUNDWATER. Water standing in or moving through the soil and underlying strata.

HABITAT. The place where an organism lives and its surroundings.

HERBIVORE. Any organism that eats only vegetation.

HETEROTROPHIC. Obtaining nutrients from organic substances.

HORIZON. A layer of soil approximately parallel to the soil surface, with distinct characteristics produced by soil-forming processes.

HUMUS. Organic matter in a more or less stable and advanced stage of decomposition, dark in color with a high nitrogen content.

HYDROLOGIC CYCLE. The cycle of movement of water from the atmosphere by precipitation to the Earth and its return to the atmosphere by evaporation and transpiration.

HYDROPHYTE. A plant that grows wholly or partly immersed in water.

HYPOTHESIS. An educated guess that forms the premise for an experiment or problem. An inference or prediction that can be tested.

INFERENCE. An educated guess based upon what has been observed about an event.

LICHEN. An alga and a fungus joined in symbiosis.

LITHOSPHERE. The Earth's crust. Soil portion of the biosphere.

LONG-DAY PLANT. A plant that blooms in long periods of light and short periods of darkness.

MESOPHYTE. A plant that grows in environmental conditions that are medium in terms of moisture.

METABOLISM. The sum total of chemical processes occurring within an organism.

MUTUALISM. Symbiosis. A relationship in which all organisms involved benefit by participation.

NICHE. The role of an organism in its environment.

NITRIC OXIDE (NO). A chemical found in photochemical smog.

NITROGEN DIOXIDE (NO_2). A chemical found in photo-chemical smog.

NITROGEN CYCLE. The circulation of nitrogen, chiefly by means of organisms, from inorganic nitrogen in the atmosphere, to nitrates, into proteins and protoplasm in plants and animals, to ammonia, and its return to nitrites and nitrates.

NUTRIENT (for plants). Any substance absorbed by a plant that is used in its metabolism.

OBSERVATION. A method, using the five senses, of studying scientific or natural phenomena.

OMNIVORE. Any animal that eats both plants and flesh.

ORGANIC. Refers to living or life forms.

ORGANIC MATTER. Materials derived from plants and ani-mals, much of it in a more or less advanced stage of decomposition.

ORGANISM. Any living thing.

OZONE (O_3). An active form of oxygen.

PARASITISM. The symbiotic interaction in which one organ-ism benefits and the other is harmed. The parasite benefits; the host organism is injured.

PEROXYACYL NITRATES (PAN). Oxides of nitrogen, nitric oxide (NO), and nitrogen dioxide (NO_2).

PARTICULATES. Particles floating in the atmosphere or in water.

PHOTOPERIODISM. The response of plants and animals to the relative duration of light and darkness.

PHOTOSYNTHESIS. The synthesis of carbohydrates from car-bon dioxide and water by chlorophyll, using light as energy, with oxygen as a by-product.

PHYSICAL. Refers to nonliving components on the Earth (air, water, soil, and light energy).

PIONEER COMMUNITY. Any of many of the successional stages on the way to a climax community. Consists of all the plants and animals in that temporary community.

POLYCHLORINATED BIPHENYLS (PCBs). Persistent poisonous chemicals released via the industrial process. Thought to be cancer-causing. Found in plastics.

PRODUCER. An organism that can utilize radiant energy to synthesize organic substances from inorganic materials.

RUN-OFF. The part of precipitation that flows off the land as surface run-off without sinking into the soil, and the part that enters the ground and passes into surface streams as groundwater run-off.

SHORT-DAY PLANT. A plant that blooms when periods of light are short and periods of darkness are long.

SMOG (photochemical). A polluted atmosphere in which the products of combustion, such as hydrocarbons, soot, and sulfur compounds, react with sunlight to form PAN and ozone.

SOIL. The aggregate of weathered minerals and decaying organic matter that covers the Earth in a thin layer in which plants grow.

SUCCESSION (ecological). The replacement of one kind of community by another kind; the progressive changes in vegetation and in animal life, which may culminate in a climax community.

SYMBIOSIS. A close relationship between two or more organisms (mutualism, commensalism, parasitism).

TEMPERATURE INVERSION. An increase in the air temperature with an increase of altitude, instead of the normal decrease.

THERMODYNAMICS, LAWS OF. (1) Energy cannot be created or destroyed but can be transferred and transformed; (2) Transformation of energy is accompanied by dispersal of a part into nonavailable heat (loss of energy), such as in respiration; (3) Absolute zero temperature is not attainable.

UNDERGROWTH. Collectively the shrubs, sprouts, seedlings, sapling trees, and all herbaceous plants in a forest.

UNDERSTORY. Collectively the trees in a forest below the upper canopy cover.

VEGETATION. Plants in general, or the sum total of plant life in an area.

WOODLAND. Any land used for growth of trees and shrubs, such as permanent woodland cover and plantings along roadsides and stream banks.

XEROPHYTE. A plant that can grow in dry places.

ZOOPLANKTON. Animals occuring in plankton (microscopic aquatic plant life.)

INDEX

Acidity-alkalinity, 87
Adaptation, 101, 112
Aerosol pollution, 31, 112
Air, makeup of, 29–31
Air pollution, 38
American elm, 103
Arctic tundra, 6–7
Atmosphere, 2–3, 112
Automobile emission, 38–45
Autotrophic component, 3
Autotrophs, 112

Biological, 112
Biological clocks, 104–106
Biomass, 4, 112
Biomes, 4–8, 112
Biosphere, 1, 2–4, 112
    biological (organic) part,
    3
    physical part, 2–3 .
Biophenyls, polychlorinated,
    79, 117
Biotic community, 2, 4, 112
Birds of prey, 103
Boreal forest, 7, 11

Carbohydrates, 100
Carbon, 100
Carbon cycle, 113

Carbon dioxide, 32, 45, 100
Carbon monoxide, 32
Carnivores, 10, 113
Carrying capacity, 11, 113
Carson, Rachel, 79
Cellulose, 113
Chaparral biome, 8, 113
Chlorinated hydrocarbons,
    77–79, 113
Chlorophyll, 113
Circadian rhythms, 113
Classified data, 27
Climax, 113
Commensalism, 102, 113
Community, 113
Conclusions, 14, 28
Condensation, 21
Coniferous forest, 5
Coniferous taiga, 7
Consumers, 99
Controlled experiment, 19
Convection, 31, 113
Convection currents, 113
Critical day length, 105

Day-neutral plant, 105, 114
DDE, 78
DDT, 77–79, 109, 114
Deciduous forest, 4, 5, 6, 114

Decomposers, 10
Desert, 4, 5, 114
Detrital food web, 10, 99–100, 114
Diversity, 101

Ecological research projects, 15, 77
Ecology, 1–2, 114
Ecosystems, 8–9, 114
Egocentric behavior, 92
Emotional behavior, 92
Energy, 110, 114
Environment, 114
Environment system, 92–99
    observation and experimentation, 99–104
Environmental project, identifying, 18–19
Equinox, 104
Eutrophic, 114
Evaporation, 2, 21
Experimentation, 28
Exponential growth, 114

First Law of Thermodynamics, 3
Food, 110
Food web, 9–11, 114
Food web detrital, 99–100, 114
Forest fire pollution, 36–38
Forest Service, 18
Formal report, 27–28
Fourdrinier, 89

Gas generator, 50
Gaseous pollution, 31
Glucose, 99
Grassland, 5, 7–8, 114
Grasslike plant, 115
Green plants, 9
Groundwater, 21, 115

Habitat, 3, 9, 103, 115
Herbivores, 10, 99, 115
Heterotrophic component, 3, 115
Homogeneous communities, 101
Horizons, 84, 115
Housing, 110-111
Human population and the environment, 107–111
Humus, 115
Hydrocarbons, chlorinated, 77–79, 113
Hydrogen sulfide, 32
Hydrologic cycle, 2, 21, 74, 115
Hydrophytes, 19, 53, 115
Hypothesis, 14, 21, 28, 115

Industrial Revolution, 107, 109
Industry, effect on water, 72–77
Inference, 14, 27, 115
Inversion, temperature, 31, 46, 117
Ionosphere, 29

Jordan machine, 89

Leaching, 87
Lichen, 102, 115
Light, response to, 105
Limiting factors of environment, 11
Lithosphere, 115
Long-day plants, 105, 115

Magma, 32
Mesophytes, 19, 53, 115
Metabolism, 115
Moisture-gradient box, 53–58
Mulch, 8

Municipalities, effect on
   water, 74–77
Mutualism, 102, 115

National Wildlife Federation,
   18
Natural gas, 100
Niche, 3, 9, 116
Nitric oxide, 32, 116
Nitrogen cycle, 29, 116
Nitrogen dioxide, 32, 116
Nutrient, 116

Observation, 13, 27, 116
Omnivore, 10, 99, 116
Organic, 116
Organic matter, 116
Organism, 116
Ozone, 32, 116

Paper, recycling, 88–91
Parasitism, 102–103, 116
Particulate pollution, 31, 116
PCBs, 79
Peroxyacyl nitrates (PAN), 116
Pesticides and water pollu-
   tion, 77–81
pH, 87
Photochemical smog, 45–50
Photoperiodic catagories, 105
Photoperiodism, 104, 116
Photosynthesis, 3, 9–10, 31,
   100, 103, 116
Physical, 116
Phytoplankton, 58
Pioneer community, 116
Pioneer stages, 58
Plain, 5
Pollution
   aerosol, 31, 112
   air, 31–32, 38
   gaseous, 31

particulate, 31, 116
volcanic, 32–36
Polychlorinated biphenyls
   (PCBs), 79, 117
Polysaccharides, 100
Population (human) and the
   environment, 107–111
Prairie, 5
Precipitation, 2, 21
Predation, 102
Predators, 10
Prediction, 14, 27
Producer, 9, 117
Pulp-making, 89

Renaissance, 109
Research, 27
Resource use-recycling pa-
   per, 88–91
Respiratory process, 100
Results, 14, 28
Rhythms, 106
Riffles, 66
River ecosystems, 65–72
Run-off, 117

Science fairs, applying to, 17–
   18
Science project, setting up
   and presenting, 19–26
Scientific method, 13–17
Second Law of Thermody-
   namics, 3
Sewage, effect on water, 75
Short-day plants, 105, 117
Sierra Club, 18
Smog, 45–50, 117
Social behavior, 92
Soil, 117
Soil and terrestrial ecosys-
   tems, 83–106
Soil formation, 83

Solstice, 104
Specific heat, 20
Stomata, 100
Stratosphere, 29
Succession, 58–65, 117
Sulfur dioxide, 31, 32
Surface water, 21
Symbiosis, 101, 117

Taiga, 7, 113
Temperate deciduous forest biome, 4, 6
Temperature inversion, 31, 46, 117
Thermodynamics, laws of, 3, 117
Transpiration, 2
Transportation, as cause of smog, 45

Tropical rain forest, 5, 6
Tundra, 5

Undergrowth, 117
Understory, 118

Vegetation, 118
Vulcanic pollution, 32–36

Water
    effect of industry on, 72–77
    physical properties, 20
    projects on, 20–26
Water vapor, 31
Woodland, 118

Xerophytes, 4, 19, 53, 118

Zooplankton, 58, 118